...dor don't forget to look up....

£3.99

11A

wk 21

Britney
spears
fan fight
30/8

Copyright © 2013 Oh Really Creative Solutions Ltd t/a Word of Mouth Travels
Editors: Owen O'Leary & Claudia Monteiro

Original 'The Locals' Guide to...' concept as realised in The Locals' Guide to Edinburgh:
Owen O'Leary and Claudia Monteiro

Writers & Contributors: Anne McMeekin, Owen O'Leary, Claudia Monteiro, Julie McIntosh

Book Design: Claire Dowling and Martin Elden

Portraits and Photography by Matthew James Reid and Chris Gillies except on pages;
2 (© Helen M Bushe), 8 (© Greg Neate), 12 (© Alan McAteer), 17 & 102 (© Graeme Bird),
21 (© Annie Flint), 26 (© Andy Cumming), 28 & 116 (© Victoria Stewart), 35 (© Kirsty Orr),
69 (© Adrian Maldonado), 74(© Phil Dunsmore), 84 (© Catherine Grant) 88 (© James B Brown),
91(© Dale Harvey), 101 (© Stevie Spiers) 107 (© Gareth Morgan) 108 (© Laura Waddell),
112 (© Scott Ferguson), 119 (© Claire Dowling)
Poem 'Clydegrad' © Edwin Morgan from Collected Poems 1996 Carcanet Press Ltd
A Word in Your Ear selection (© Michael Munro) chosen from The Complete Patter 2007 Birlinn Ltd
Illustration Copyright: Front cover icon Eva Dolgyra. Inside cover & pg 118 (© Nora Reid),
pg 31 (© Mhari Baxter), pg 59 (© Anna Kraay), page 62, 120, 131, 132, 134 (© Eva Dolgyra)
pg 64 (© Essi Kimpimäki)

First published in Great Britain in November 2013 by Oh Really Creative Solutions Ltd
t/a Word of Mouth Travels

Oh Really Creative Solutions Ltd t/a
Word of Mouth Travels
6/2 Rosebank
Edinburgh EH5 3QN
www.wordofmouthtravels.co.uk

ISBN 978-0-9557529-1-9

Still reading this? Come on, there's a whole city waiting for you. Get stuck in!

The Locals' Guide to

Glasgow

word of mouth travels

2014-2015

CONTENTS

This is Glasgow.

Scotland's largest city is the western world in miniature.
Large, loud and lots of fun. Where parks, museums and architecture
are everywhere. Proud of its social conscience. Shaped by a
socialist past.

Go for a wander round Kelvingrove Museum, its beautiful
gothic architecture smiles warmly over the West End hosting
a wealth of egalitarian riches bought by the people, for the
people. Muddle through hoards of city centre shoppers on
a Saturday afternoon, past dapper old timers off to the bingo,

LET·GLASGOW·FLOURISH

proudly strutting side by side with upstart fashionistas in their granny's vintage cast offs.

Take a peek (if you dare) into the market maze of the Barras and aye you'll probably find that bootleg album you've been hunting for but you'll also find a hundred folk working hard to earn a living the only way they know how – their patter. If you leave empty handed you'll be stronger of mind than most.

Venture out at night and take a drink with the locals – you might just stumble across the next big thing playing a gig or putting on a show in someone's back room, about to join the long list of Glasgow's cultural aristocracy. If you're luckier you'll find some new pals propping up the

bar, entertaining you 'til the wee hours with tall tales and fantastic fables that will be told and retold for generations to come.

From the arching leafy terraces of Hyndland to the shipyards of Govan; from the sophisticated wine bars to the gaudy, flashing signs of the Barrowland Ballroom – welcome to Glasgow! City of music, city of art, city of culture, city of good times, city of a thousand songs (and a thousand people singing along).

Mon' over and join in, we want to tell you a story…

What this book is about

We often wander around cities wishing we had a good friend to show us around, someone who could filter out the obvious and take us to the heart of a place. A guide that makes you feel at home in a city you've only just arrived in. And then the promise of our getaway suddenly comes true: we find ourselves in the middle of a dance hall trying to follow those unattainable local rhythms; savouring a cocktail on a rooftop restaurant; chatting to locals in a busy backstreet pub, having someone tempt us to romantic strolls and a spot of stargazing. If you want to immerse yourself under the skin of the city, whether you'll be here for a day or a decade, then keep reading. This is the book for you.

We've asked everyone we know in Glasgow to tell us exactly what makes home special; which eateries, bars, shops and walks they absolutely couldn't live without.

And then we asked some more. We invited 'local legends' to guide you through the city, and they'll be speaking directly to you from the pages of the book. Whether you're a visitor who does not want to do the 'tourist trail', or a local resident who is willing to try some new things, take their word for it and check out their stories, tips and thoughts.

Welcome to Glasgow, enjoy!

p.s. – We have a no advertising policy. Instead, places are featured on merit alone, either because they're unique, inspiring or run by people who genuinely care about their trade. This book has been written, designed and photographed by Glasgow based folk and those in love with city.

GLASGOW U

MAP O

Kelvingrove Park
Western Infirmary
Yorkhill Hospital
Queen Mother's Hospital
Glasgow Museum & Art Galleries
Kelvin Hall Sports Complex
Kelvin Hall Transport Museum

Glasgow University
Hunterian Museum
BBC Studios
Botanical Gardens
Byres Road

Kelvin Walkway
Queen's College

Partick Station
Partick Burgh Hall
Partick Bus Station

HILLHEAD U

KELVINBRIDGA
U

KELVIN HALL

PARTICK U

GOVAN U

IBROX U

CESSNOCK U

KINNING PARK
U

SHIELD

Pearce Institute
Bus Station

Ibrox Stadium
Govan Town Hall

Paisley Road West
Palace of Art
Bellahouston Park

Scotland St

Strath
Transp

Loop the loop. The subway will have you going around in
more so thanks to Greg Neate for spotting it and our d

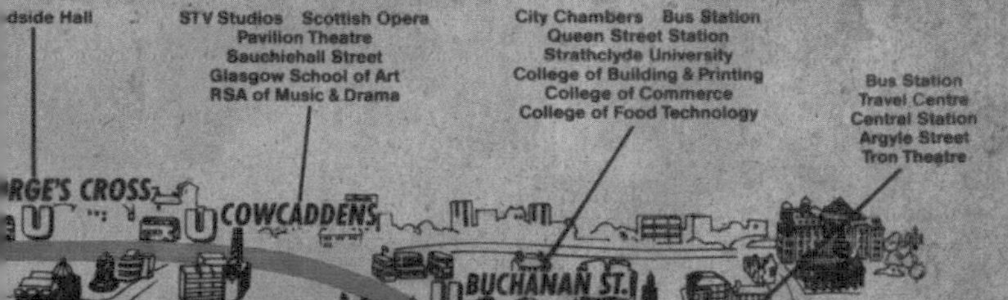

dside Hall

STV Studios   Scottish Opera
Pavilion Theatre
Sauchiehall Street
Glasgow School of Art
RSA of Music & Drama

City Chambers   Bus Station
Queen Street Station
Strathclyde University
College of Building & Printing
College of Commerce
College of Food Technology

Bus Station
Travel Centre
Central Station
Argyle Street
Tron Theatre

RGE'S CROSS

U

U COWCADDENS

BUCHANAN ST.

ST. ENOCH

BRIDGE STREET

WEST STREET

U

Sheriff Court
Citizens Theatre
Mosque

U

s in a good way. They don't make maps like this one any
r Martin Elden for giving it the treatment it deserves!

Read it and weep.
The stunning interior of Glasgow School of Art's Library
designed by Charles Rennie Mackintosh

NEIGHBOURHOODS
(A few words about a few places)

City Centre

From the most eastern tip of Argyle Street up to where Sauchiehall Street meets Charing Cross, Glasgow's compact city centre is halted bluntly to the west where the monolithic Kingston Bridge cuts through the city like an aggressive artery. The area is a brash mix of shoppers, shops and shopping centres, bars and restaurants, train stations and hotels, office blocks and industry, with chic shop assistants, hectic businessmen and day tripping pensioners all jostling for position on Buchanan Street. Despite the regular grid system it's worth keeping an eye on street signs, as even hardened locals can find themselves wandering aimlessly up streets parallel to their required location.

Merchant City

From Ingram Street to Bridgegate, the Merchant City sits to the east of the city centre like a more sensible and stylish older sister, an always tasteful mix of old and new, distinguished architecture and modern design, history and history in the making. At its heart lies The Old Fruitmarket, a lovingly restored space for concerts and events surrounded by independent boutiques, swanky bars and cool cafés. Steeped in rich trading history, the Merchant City has emerged as the jewel in Glasgow's crown after years of regeneration.

West End

The towering gothic spires of Glasgow University point upwards, towards the infinite sky, reaching for the heavens like the aspirational residents of the West End. The neighbourhood hosts a mix of students, coffee drinking yummy mummies and intellectuals on their way to the library. From the regal townhouses atop Park Circus to the palatial flats on the leafy streets of Hyndland, the area

is a green respite to the harsh concrete of the city centre. Along Byres Road and Great Western Road independent shops, cute cafés, intellectual hang outs and trendy bars line the pavements. A stroll along side streets reveal beautiful bay windows yawning in the sunlight, giving you a peek at how the other half live.

Southside

To the south of the Clyde the city becomes predominantly residential amidst remnants of Glasgow's trading past, with converted warehouses giving way to new builds and grand old tenements still standing tall. The Southside envelops routes leading out of the city centre towards Shawlands. The area has established itself as an enclave to be reckoned with for Glasgow's more sensible young professionals, whether you're looking for a dress, a nice meal or a quick cup of coffee. It is also home to two of Glasgow's best parks: the award-winning Pollock Country Park and Queen's Park, complete with its own Reptile House sitting high above Pollockshaws Road.

East End

To the eastern limits of Merchant City sits High Street and the beginnings of the East End where the finesse ends abruptly and Glasgow's tougher side emerges. Once a driving hub of industry, the East End has experienced a sharp decline in its fortunes with many once prestigious buildings now fallen into disrepair. Regeneration in the city has been creeping slowly eastward and residential areas such as Dennistoun are being populated by the mandatory coffee shops and delicatessens while many tourists will be drawn to popular attractions such as the People's Palace and The Barras Market.

Dear Green Place,

We would like to stay:
one night / a weekend / a week / forever

somewhere that's:
cheap / stylish / different / welcoming

can you give us tips to:
whet our accommodation appetite / get us
excited about Glasgow / start our trip in style

Yours in anticipation...

_____ x

■Glasgow Youth Hostel　□15　▯Pipers' Tryst

Budget accommodation without budging on standards...

Set in one of the city's most exclusive addresses the **Glasgow Youth Hostel** in the West End sits around the corner from the stunning townhouses of Park Circus. Five minutes from Kelvingrove with stunning views across the city, it's not just cheap and cheerful but characterful and charming too! (Glasgow Youth Hostel, 8 Park Terrace, West End t: 0141 332 3004, Map B2)

As part of the Scottish Piping Centre, the **Pipers' Tryst** is less budget than a hostel but well worth the slightly extra spend for a slice of Scottish heritage. Set in a converted church in the city centre this restaurant with rooms features piper portraits throughout. A different tartan on every floor, thick walls and cosy rooms mean even if the pipes are calling you'll not hear them. (Pipers' Tryst, 30 – 34 McPhater Street, City Centre t: 0141 353 5551, Map B3)

B+B should never stand for boring and bland but too often it does. Steer clear of the mundane and go for these braw* and barry** options...

The attention to detail in **15 Glasgow** is incredible. This luxury boutique bed and breakfast goes above and beyond the call of duty with monsoon showers, feather pillows and underfloor heating in the en suite bathrooms. Owners Laura and Shane have struck the perfect balance between contemporary style and Victorian grandeur. (15 Glasgow, 15 Woodside Place, West End t: 0141 332 1263, Map B2)

In what could be mistaken for marks out of 1900, **1883 Guesthouse** is a lovely sandstone building in the Southside. Hosted by Bill and Lorna and their dog Charlie, this welcoming home is a chance to sample top Scottish hospitality first hand. (1883 Guesthouse, 58 Glenapp Street, Southside t: 07775 832461, Map D3)

*fine, splendid **good, wonderful

For those wanting the best of city and country style accommodation, head to **The Flower House**. A lush green entrance makes way for a welcoming B&B right in the heart of the city. Striking distance from the city centre and the West End, Susan and Ian's Victorian home can be yours too. (33 St Vincent Crescent, West End, t: 0141 204 2846, Map C2)

Taking care of business / pleasure / shopping stopovers, these switched on spots have got the savvy traveller scene all sewn up.

citizenM Glasgow has über-style as standard. Every room is exactly the same filled by an XL bed, Vitra furniture and shower pod and all controlled by a mood board tablet. For the tech savvy, footloose and design conscious CitizenM has it all. Mmmm... (60 Renfrew Street, City Centre t: 0141 404 9485, Map B3)

Just a (grass)hop skip and jump from the platforms of Glasgow Central is **Grasshoppers Penthouse Hotel**. Scandinavian styling meets Scottish hospitality in this 30 room modern hotel. Don't be deceived by the entrance way and ascend to new heights of affordable luxury. (87 Union Street, City Centre t: 0141 222 2666, Map C3)

Scotland with style? Rest at the best for a beautiful stay

The danger of staying at **The Blythswood Hotel** is that you might never make it out to explore Glasgow. This once private club of the Scottish Automobile Association has been restored to its former glory and more. Plush, personable and full of treats, make sure you stay long enough to enjoy it all. (11 Blythswood Square, City Centre t: 0141 240 1666, Map B3)

◻ Glasgow Holiday Cottage ◻ Blythswood Square ▢ citizenM

ALAN

Interview:
Alan Pert
(Architect)

> Unlike other British cities,
> Glasgow draws its influences
> from cities like Chicago, San
> Francisco and grand European
> capitals – the geometric grid
> and the grand boulevards.
> Details such as the elevation
> of buildings and the statues of
> the city speak of an amazing
> history – one of recognition of
> Glasgow's position globally at
> the turn of the 20th century, an

urban force that was at the heart of the Empire.

One of the greatest forces shaping the city are its people and the rich social infrastructure put in place during Victorian times. I've got this great nostalgia about the architecture of that period, which goes beyond the grand elements in places like Green Park or the People's Palace – I'm talking about the social infrastructure in daily life, things like the railings, the street lighting, the signage and public toilets.

Some of the most iconic symbols of the British Empire were manufactured in this city: the ships that sustained trade and military power, Singer machines, the notorious red phonebox, tram sheds and the teahouse pavilions that were so fashionable at the time – people used to meet up for afternoon tea in them in places as far as India!

Streets nowadays have become a bit generic and we face the danger of having every city in Britain looking all too familiar. But in Victorian Glasgow there was a real sense of collective pride and craftsmanship about what came out of factories and workshops. This understanding of materials is something that's

visible in bars like Rogano or The Steps Bar, where you can admire the level of craft built into the walls and furnishings. Even if you don't need to go, visit the public toilets on St Vincent Street, which are the last remaining example in the city from the Victorian era.

Imagine thousands of people working in manufacturing under the same roof, coming together to produce this one same thing. As a day-to-day experience it breeds a kind of sociability amongst Glaswegians which still shapes the city's identity; the reputation for good chat and conviviality that's well and truly alive in Glasgow today.

Check Alan Pert's latest work on www.nordarchitecture.com

See The Locals' Directory on page 136 for Alan's top tips.

Heaven sent, **Malmaison Glasgow** has transformed an Episcopalian Church into a very different place of worship. Decadent styling, a buzzing bar and all the little touches that make a stayover special. Amen to that. (278 West George Street, City Centre t: 0844 693 0653, Map B3)

Really want to feel at home in Glasgow?
Then look after your self catering here:

Fancy being a West End local? Hidden down the leafy streets of Partick is the **Glasgow Holiday Cottage**. Hosts Roger and Annie have created the perfect city hideaway. Tasteful touches of retro enhance this lovely one bedroom cottage with its own private patio area. (2 Banavie Rd, West End, t: 0141 357 6705, Map A1)

Nestling on the edge of the Merchant City and East End are the **Tolbooth Apartments**. With views of the Tolbooth steeple these modern stylish open plan apartments put you in the heart of the action without hearing any of it. Underground parking, free wifi and superb service from Ronnie and his team get these the self catering seal of approval. (12/24 High St, Merchanct City, t: 0141 404 0086, Map C4)

Hey, big spender!

Have it all at **Mar Hall**. This 53 room sumptuous golf and spa resort overlooking the Clyde is the straight out of a period drama. Set in 260 acres of stunning grounds and restored to its former Edwardian glory in 2004, Mar Hall is for when luxury matters. (Mar Hall Drive, Bishopton, Nr Glasgow, 20 minutes from city centre, t: 0141 812 9999)

More than just the Old Firm,
Glasgow's four teams get represented in an airing on Glasgow Green.
(L-R) Queens Park, Partick Thistle, Rangers and Celtic.

INTERVIEW: Petra Wetzel

(Bavarian Brewster)

From studying Politics, French and Art History at Glasgow University to brewing lagers and wheat beers on Glasgow Green, Bavarian Petra Wetzel is thinking global but acting like a local.

I came to Glasgow as a student, not knowing yet it would become my home. I feel like a local but it's great to have the added benefit of viewing the city with outsider's eyes. I used to work for the Glasgow Tourist Board and always took people to see slices of the real Glasgow rather than just sticking to the main attractions.

The idea to set up a brewery came to me in 1994, when my dad was visiting from Bavaria and wanted to try the local beer. He was surprised there wasn't one and that's when the plan was born. In March 2006 the plan became a reality and we opened up in the beautiful Templeton Building on Glasgow Green.

Petra looks to the future through the big windows at Box of Delights

The city has plenty of amazing buildings but this former carpet factory based on the original Doges Palace in Venice is the perfect blend of Glasgow's work and style ethic. The brewery is a great combination of German traditions and Scottish ingenuity and St Mungo's, our lager, has won a host of brewing awards.

When I manage to sneak out of the brewery I love nothing more than embracing the green open spaces close to the city. As a dog owner and mum to a young son the parks are a big draw. The Kelvin Walkway to the Botanic Gardens is a real Saturday morning favourite haunt of mine; my son Noah likes to stop at the fish pond in the Kibble Palace along the way – and we've spent many rainy days sitting on a bench in the big glass house reading stories.

We love going to Pollock Country Park (and its delightful tearoom) in the Southside and, further out, Mugdock Country Park near our house is the perfect weekend getaway. Oh, and if you get the chance you must check out the Glasgow's Farmer Market which moves between Partick and Queens Park, depending on the week. For eating out it has to be to be Mother India, the best curry house in town, the Crabshakk for 5pm champagne and oysters or The Left Bank for its laid back atmosphere. If I'm out and about you'll find me in Bar 91 and sometimes at Cottier's Theatre - a converted church in the West End where I can bring my Golden Retriever Heidi.

The perfect morning-after the night before breakfast can be had at a little caf called Box of Delights on the corner of Ingram St and Candleriggs. I'll see you there at 7.30am! Coffee and poached eggs on toast is only £2.50!

See The Locals' Directory page 136 for Petra's top tips.

Clydegrad

by Edwin Morgan

It was so fine we lingered there for hours.

The long broad streets shone strongly after rain.

Sunset blinded the tremble of the crane
we watched from, dazed the heliport-towers.

The mile-high buildings flashed, flushed, greyed, went dark,

greyed, flushed, flashed, chameleons under flak

of cloud and sun. The last far thunder-sack

ripped and spilled its grumble. Ziggurat-stark,

a power-house reflected in the lead

of the old twilight river leapt alive

lit up at every window, and a boat

of students rowed past, slid from black to red

into the blaze. But where will they arrive

with all, boat, city, earth, like them, afloat?

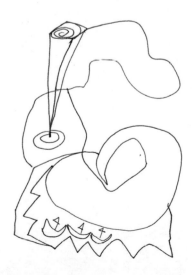

Food, friends and family.

It's all about bringing people together. Glasgow's unique gastronomic geography showcases the finest foods from around the world. A destination for curry lovers as much as a home for health food fanatics, the city takes worldwide influences and serves them up in style whether it's in fine dining surrounds or a street food setting. Amongst the curry houses, Italian restaurants and locally sourced superstars are eateries of all shapes and sizes waiting to wow you. So take your time and treat your tastebuds...

❒Café Rio   ❒Babu Bombay Kitchen   ❒Gusto and Relish

Wake up to some good food. Morning rolls, healthy porridge, traditional Scottish or design on a plate?

Gusto and Relish seems intent on turning breakfast into an art form. This excellent Strathbungo café/deli isn't messing with the much loved fry up, with the emphasis on quality sausages and fluffy potato scones, it's just doing it much better. (weekdays from 9.30am, saturday from 10am, sunday from 11am, 729 Pollokshaws Rd, Southside, t: 0141 424 1233, Map D3)

Does anywhere capture the spirit of Merchant City better than **Brutti ma Buoni**? We don't think so. It's favoured by the conspicuously cool but a refreshingly mixed crowd also enjoy the hangover zapping breakfasts. Ask for poached eggs and you won't regret it. (daily from 11am, 106 Brunswick St, City Centre, t: 0141 552 0001, Map C4)

For an old fashioned "full Scottish" look no further than the **University Café**. This chippie cum ice cream parlour cum diner is a Glasgow institution – it's been run by the Verrecchia family since 1918. Squeeze up beside the locals and listen in. (monday to saturday from 9am, sunday from 10am, 87 Byres Rd, West End, t: 0141 339 5217, Map A1)

NYC comes to Partick with **Tribeca**, a taste of American breakfast heaven. Pancakes, smoothies, eggs anyway-you-like and the most reasonably priced bacon bagels this side of the Hudson. (weekdays from 9am, weekends from 10am, 102 Dumbarton Rd, West End, t: 0141 576 0122, Map B1)

Step into Happy Days at **Café Rio** where Formica tables and 50's retro booths house giggling pals and hungover lovers refuelling on breakfast staples with an upmarket twist. Think eggs Florentine and chips washed down with some of the best milkshakes in Glasgow. Yum. (Monday to Sunday from 9am, 27 Hyndland St, West End, t: 0141 334 9909 B1)

Dashing out or dining in. These places make lunch the most important meal of the day.

The Horseshoe Bar is a living, breathing, unreconstructed Glasgow legend. Every section of the city's society is represented here at lunchtime. Join them and enjoy three courses for the price of a deli ciabatta. (daily from 11am, 17 Drury Lane, City Centre, t: 0141 229 5711, Map C3)

Heart Buchanan is a favourite with Glasgow's West Enders. Fabulous salads, soups, sandwiches, pasta, chicken and fish dishes all served to stay or go in bright, bustling surroundings. Also offers popular cookery classes. (monday to friday from 8.30am, saturday from 9am and sunday from 12noon, 380 Byres Rd, West End, t: 0141 334 7626, Map A2)

Fresh Express! **Martha's** has livened up lunchtime in the city centre with fast natural food. From Superfreak salads to Red Dragon Pork dishes, their heroic menu championing local produce puts the 'Hell yeah!' into healthy eating. (monday to friday from 7:30am-4pm, saturday from 11am-4pm, closed sunday, 142a St. Vincent Street, City Centre, t: 0141 248 9711, Map C3)

Slap bang in the middle of the East End, the family-run **Eusebi Deli** alone merits the trip to Shettleston. The customers who come from far and wide for the amazing bread, olives, meats, cheese seafood, pasta and cakes seem to think so. (monday to saturday from 9am, closed Sunday, 793 Shettleston Rd, East End, t: 0141 763 0399, Map beyond B4)

Thanks to **Babu Bombay Kitchen** you don't have to travel thousands of miles for superb Indian street food. Chappatis, Curry 3 ways and a Dhal of the Day for lentil lovers are just a hearty handful of reasons to make a trip to Bombay a daily occurrence. (monday to friday from 7am-6pm, saturday from 10am-6pm, closed sunday, 186 West Regent Street, City Centre, t: 0141 204 4042, Map C3)

A Glasgow lunch staple, **Where the Monkey Sleeps** has been serving up delicious(ly cool) sandwiches in its subterranean street art alcoves for nearly a decade. Despite some of the oddest names ever given to a sandwich (Mr Bolland's Cutlass anyone?), the only surprise on this menu is that the food really is as interesting and delicious as its description. (monday to friday from 7am-4pm, 182 West Regent St, City Centre, t: 0141 376 8783, Map C3)

Tom Lauckner and John Moore have made something special with **Piece**. For this gourmet sandwich shop something special is always on the menu. With sister shops popping up across town,wherever you're going in Glasgow may Piece be with you. (monday to friday from 8am-6pm, saturday from 10am-6pm, closed sunday,1056 Argyle St, West End, t: 0141 221 7975, Map B2)

◖Martha's ◖The Horseshoe Bar ◖Eusebi Deli

Please come again

Harry gets into the swing of things in *The Three Judges*

Harry is now part of the team at the Riverside Museum but we caught up with him just before he left the Kelvingrove Museum and Art Gallery.

❝ ❝ I took the job at the Kelvingrove Museum in 1992, after a career change. It was purely accidental, but if I'd known before how much I would enjoy working here I would have become a visitor assistant straight after school. I get to meet people from all walks of life and from different countries – that is the best part of my work.

This place is incredibly friendly and great for children. And so many Glasgwegians have good memories of Kelvingrove; in the old days couples would use the gallery for courting. There is so much to take in that I would suggest to people to do it in sections: if you live in Glasgow come here every now and again and spend some time exploring the different exhibitions.

I have got my own favourites: the Scottish Colourists, who represent an important moment for painting in Scotland; and the furniture designers who designed the Tea Rooms that were so popular in Glasgow. The Scottish Identity exhibition is really educational too, and if you want to learn about the myths and stories of our history - from the Battle of Glencoe to the role of tartan memorabilia – then this exhibition is really entertaining.

There are some other wonderful museums to visit in Glasgow. I recommend The Tenement House, as it's kept all the Victorian fixtures and fittings of a working family home and for some stunning architecture take a look into the City Chambers. Then there is the absolutely wonderful Glasgow School of Art, which was designed and furnished by Charles Rennie Mackintosh – it feels like a living museum really. And of course, no trip to Glasgow is complete without a visit to the Riverside.

When I've got Sunday afternoons off you'll find me in The Three Judges pub, their resident jazz group Muldoon's Rag Time Band entertains regulars with some really good music. So as we say in the museum, please come again!"

See The Locals' Directory page 136 for Harry's top tips.

Dining out without dressing up needn't be a let down. Try these top tips for casual comfort eating.

Award winning **Tibo** might be off the main drag but it's well worth a visit. Chock full of bistro favourites the menu will please veggies and carnivores alike. Still something of an undiscovered treat – go now. (443 Duke St, East End, t: 0141 550 2050, Map C4)

Glasgow is famed for its curry houses. The much loved **Mother India** sits at the top of this tree delivering stylish food (spiced haddock starter is a highlight) in surroundings to match. The fact that it's a BYOB with corkage for buttons only heightens the appeal. (28 Westminster Terr, West End/City Centre border, t: 0141 221 1663, Map B2)

Serving simple healthy Japanese food **Ichiban Sushi and Noodle Bar** is the perfect place for city sit in. Join other diners on their long tables and share the slurps of appreciation and oohs of pleasant surprise as the bills arrive. Also on Dumbarton Road in the West End. (50 Queen Street, Merchant City t: 0141 204 4200, Map C3)

More people should know about **The Cabin Restaurant**, which has the look and air of a familial front room. The stupendous Scottish/Irish cuisine is almost an aside when faced with musical owner Denis Dwyer. He leads the patrons in a nightly sing song. It might sound naff, but it's not. This is a one off in a location few out of towners ever visit. (996 Dumbarton Rd, West End fringes, t: 0141 569 1036, Map A1)

Searching for a great French restaurant? Step forward **La Valle Blanche** which has won fans all over the place with its concise seasonal menu of Gallic favourites. (360 Byres Rd, West End, t: 0141 334 3333, Map A1)

For feel good and pho good eating get down to Glasgow's first Vietnamese restaurant the **Hanoi Bike Shop**. With dishes ideal for sharing this casual vibrant setting places an emphasis on fresh and fantastic food. (8 Ruthven Lane, West End, t: 0141 334 7165, Map A1)

When eating is an occasion...

Scotland's produce gets chefs jumping with joy. If you can't afford dinner, then do not miss out on the lunch offers - you can be eating food fit for the Gods for heavenly prices. Booking is essential.

Opened in 1935, **Rogano** is Glasgow's oldest surviving restaurant and arguably its best. This art deco homage to the great Queen Mary liner, serves up some of the finest seafood and meat around. In fact, it would be difficult to find a bad choice on the menu of classics. Join the city's slickers, stick on your best frock and order a cocktail. (11 Exchange Pl, City Centre, t: 0141 248 4055, Map C3)

Crabshakk has taken Glasgow's restaurant scene by storm. And rightly so. This seafood temple offers a mouth watering array of dishes from individual oysters to whole lobster and almost everything in between. Make sure to book ahead and beware the entrance – so discreet, it's almost invisible. (1114 Argyle St, West End/City Centre border, t: 0141 334 6127, Map B2)

Leaving the hubbub of cobbled Ashton Lane behind, stepping into the gorgeous mews that is the **Ubiquitous Chip** is a bit like entering another universe. With its towering plants and fish pond, the courtyard atmosphere is as sublime as the inventive Scottish-with-a-twist food. Braised Perthshire pig's cheek, wild mushroom sauce and truffled potato omelette, anyone? (12 Ashton Lane, West End, t: 0141 334 5007, Map A1)

Be sure to groom – spray tan, manicure and blow dry – if you plan to head for private members club **29**. This is where Glasgow's glitterati come out to play. And it's a lot of fun: from the gorgeous bar and wait staff and the twinkly view across Exchange Square to the pretty fine modern European fare. Non members can dine any night except Saturday. (29 Royal Exchange Sq, City Centre, t: 0141 225 5610, Map C3)

... and for those who care for their vegetables.

Bar/restaurant/music venue and – as befits its über cool status – there's even an independent music shop and book exchange at **Mono**. This vegan joint has appeal that stretches well beyond the tofu brigade. (everyday from 12noon, 12 Kings Court, City Centre, t: 0141 552 9458, Map C4)

Beloved of the student population, nearby The **13th Note** is another impressive meat free establishment. With live music, weekend DJs, art exhibitions and people watching opportunities it's easy to forget about the food. Don't, it's great. (everyday from noon, 50 King St, City Centre, t: 0141 553 1638, Map C3)

It's late. I mean really late. There is nothing open except...

Wind your way to **Asia Style** a delightful Chinese Malaysian diner. As the location (it looks onto the motorway) might suggest, there's no pomp here. The eclectic clientele don't seem to mind, in fact the strip lighting and interesting toilets actually heighten the appeal. Glasgow's Chinese community eat here – always a good sign. The tea is free and the food first rate – try the salt and pepper squid. (everyday till 2am, 185 St Georges Rd, West End/City Centre border, t: 0141 332 8828, Map B3)

From Toulouse sausages with basil mash to roast rabbit, the **Baby Grand**'s menu has something for everyone. And most nights, it also serves up some deliciously kitsch piano music. Indulge your inner European with some late night grub and classic tinkling. (sunday to thursday till midnight, friday and saturday till 1am, 3 Elmbank Gdns, City Centre t: 0141 248 4942 Map B3)

◖Mono ◣Crabshakk ◼Rogano

The People's Palace ☐ Hidden Lane Tearooms ☐ Moyra Janes

Before cafe culture, before high streets and before dinner, there was tea. Cuppas, cakes and chat are still the cornerstones of Glasgow's social scene. Tuck into your tea here...

It's always summer at the **Grianach Café**: the name means sunny in Gaelic and light therapy boxes adorn each table. This cute neighbourhood oasis specialises in home baking. So get your shades on and opt for the famous cup cakes. (monday to friday from 9am, saturday from 10am and sunday from 11am, 38 Nithsdale Rd, Southside, t: 0141 423 5926, Map D3)

Moyra Janes is more than a teashop. Open late 5 nights a week with homely menu and more besides this institution once famous for being the location of a Scottish Blend adverts continues to host actors at theatre nights throughout the year. Get the night right and you could be having tea with some of Scotland's best thesps. (18 – 20 Kildrostan Street, Southside, t: 0141 423 5628, Map beyond D3)

Explorers are richly rewarded at the (well) **Hidden Lane Tearoom**. Look for 1103 painted above the archway on Argyle St, through and turn left and left again for an oasis of calm and cream teas. (Mercat House, 1103 Argyle Street, West End, t: 0141 237 4391, Map C2)

Husband and wife team Phil and Claire are the **Kember and Jones** in question. Ms Jones and her team are responsible for the gorgeous selection of scones and cakes – certainly one of the reasons why this place is always mobbed. (everyday from 9am, 134 Byres Rd, West End, t: 0141 337 3851, Map A1)

The People's Palace, Glasgow's social history museum, is held in great affection by the city's residents and the attached Victorian glasshouse, the **Winter Gardens** is a gorgeous tropical paradise. Importantly, it also has a great little café where regulars rave about the Empire biscuits. (monday to thursday and saturday from 10am, friday and sunday from 11am, Glasgow Green, East End, t: 0141 276 0788, Map D4)

INTERVIEW: LIMMY
(comedian)

Limmy's comedy website attracts followers from all over the world. This is a man for whom a good cup of tea is as important as a good laugh.

It's like a jungle sometimes...
Limmy gets to grips with the flora and fauna
in the Botanic Gardens

" I grew up in Carnwadric, a council estate on the south side. It was a bit rough at times, but without that experience I wouldn't have half the ideas for characters and storylines that I do. There's something about grim situations, pessimism and bad stuff happening that can be quite humorous. Glasgow is a funny place like that: we supposedly have a self-deprecating, dark humour here that outsiders love, but I don't notice it myself – probably because I'm used to it.

My comedy plays a lot on the dark side of Glasgow, like madness and violence and hopelessness, with characters like John Paul the ultraviolent ned*, Jacqueline McCafferty the recovering junkie, and Dee Dee the dosser. Glasgow as a whole is not that downbeat, though, it's no different to any other big city, really; but that's the side I find the funniest, for whatever reason.

I stopped drinking in 2004, so I'm not as charmed by old men's pubs as much as I used to be, because I'm more into tea and biscuits nowadays. Cranberry's is a real treat. It's a tearoom with delicious cakes and old ladies aplenty. Imagine tea at your granny's, only imagine you actually wanted to be there, it's something like that. My other favourite haunt is Firebird. They do really nice pizzas and have these gigantic windows that are perfect for people watching in the summer.

I live in the West End now and love to walk by the River Kelvin. There's a half hour walk I like doing from the Botanic Gardens that goes all the way to Kelvingrove Park. Ducks, people walking their dogs, the sound of the river… it's lovely and peaceful."

* a cheeky tracksuited trouble-maker.

See The Locals' Directory page 136 for Limmy's top tips. Limmy's Show! Is available on DVD at Amazon.co.uk and for everything else check out www.limmy.com

Coffee. Stop. Coffee. Stop. Go Here...

Stripped back and spartan **Papercup** keeps things simple. A no nonsense coffee menu, some fab food and service Sydney style focuses on all the right things to bring you the bean at its best.
(Papercup, 603 Great Western Road, West End, Map A2)

Coffee, lots of different varieties of it, and hot chocolate reign supreme at **Jelly Hill**. West Enders meet to gossip in its cosy wooden interior or, on sunny days, spill out onto street side tables. The atmosphere is somewhat conspiratorial, especially when coffee leads to a glass of wine. The cakes are tip top too. (everyday from 8am, 195 Hyndland Rd, West End, t: 0141 341 0055, Map A1)

Fashion meets function in the straight lines and superb coffee at **Tinderbox**. Served with slices of Berlin, Amsterdam and Barcelona this is Scotland's coffee with style. Whether it's an alcohol free evening or a shopping pit stop this Merchant City caffeine haven is one place you've got (coffee) to go. (118 Ingram Street, Merchant City, t: 0141 552 6907, Map C4)

Serious coffee lover? Check out the fab selection of reviews on Glasgow local Dave Bennett's excellent coffee blog **www.grindmybeans.co.uk**

Whether it is the last stop on the way back from the pub or the saving grace in a stressful day, these are Glasgow's fast food favourites.

The Maggie: this cracking little food van is famed for its "Scooby Snax" - that's bacon, egg, sausage, potato scone and black pudding altogether in a roll. Get your jaws round it if you can. (weekend nights 'til 3am, outside entrance to the Botanic Gdns, West End, Map A2)

It's worth crossing Scotland, let alone Glasgow to get to this Southside hotspot. **Istanbul Turkish**'s charcoal fired ovens cook everything in front of you and firm favourites include the lamachun Turkish pizzas and the incredible kebabs. (7 Paisley Road, Southside t: 0141 429 1232, Map D2)

Go shopping and stock your pantry with some of these amazing foods...

James Allan Butchers has a reputation which stretches well beyond its Hyndland address. The prime cuts of meat, the wide selection of sausages are first rate and the steak pies are a real winner here. (monday to saturday 9am to 5.30pm, 85 Lauderdale Gdns, West End, t: 0141 334 8973, Map A1)

This place is pricey, but for restaurant standard ready meals, fresh pies, salads, breads and cakes you can't go wrong with **Delizique**. For those wanting to linger, the pizzas are a must as is a visit to sister establishment Cafezique just down the road. (monday to sunday 9am-7pm, 70 Hyndland St, West End, t: 0141 339 2000, Map A1)

Iain Mellis has been in the fromage business for 30 years. His **IJ Mellis Cheesemongers** has a brilliant range and the staff can talk for hours about variations and flavours. They'll even let you try out a wee bit before you decide what to buy. The shop itself is a gorgeous space and includes a cellar where cheese is ripened to perfection. (monday to saturday from 9.30am, IJ Mellis Cheesemongers: 492 Great Western Road, tel: 0141 339 8998, Map A2)

Doug Bell and Rhoda Robertson set up **Lupe Pintos** in Edinburgh after a trip to Mexico in 1989. Expect tortilla, chillies and tequila and a whole heap more as this place carries a wide range of Mexican, American, Spanish and Caribbean products. (sunday 12.30pm-5.30pm, monday to wednesday 10am-6pm, thursday and friday 10am-7pm, 311 Great Western Rd, West End, t: 0141 334 5444, Map A2)

At the **Glasgow Farmer's Market** you can get your chops round some of the best rural fare. Breads, meat, game, cheese, chutneys and home baking all feature – a great morning outing. (twice monthly 10am – 2pm, Southside: Queens Park 1st and 3rd saturday, West End: Mansfield Park 2nd and 4th Saturday, Map beyond D3 and B2).

◨Ichiban　◧Papercup　◻The Maggie

The Doubl

Graeme and Chris's heated curry debate comes to blows

Award-winning bloggers Graeme Virtue and Chris Cameron (AKA Trampy and The Tramp), chat about their love of curry and why Glasgow is second to none in the spicy stakes.

Two self-appointed members of Scotland's young media elite, Graeme Virtue and Chris Cameron met in Glasgow in 2000 and became fast friends, bonding over a shared love of curry and movies. Chris, in particular, was fascinated by the rich history of curry restaurants in Glasgow dating back to the 1960s – according to his dad, Chris had enjoyed his first taste of korma when he was just two years old, at the original Shish Mahal on Gibson Street.

Graeme and Chris set up their weekly blog **Trampy and The Tramp's Glasgow of Curry** (TATTGOC) in 2008, celebrating curry culture in their home city and beyond. But where does the distinctive name come from? One night, the pair ended up sharing a dessert at a restaurant. A friend said it resembled the alley dinner scene in Disney's Lady and The Tramp. "More like Trampy and The Tramp," said Graeme, and that became the inspiration for their blog.

"The original point of TATTGOC was entirely social, to meet up with a group of friends once a month and go for a curry. Everyone has their personal favourite curryhouse in Glasgow and tend to be very loyal, but we wanted to get out of our comfort zone and try places we'd never been to before. So that was our intention – to go out and discover hidden gems all over the city. We set up the blog to keep track of where we've been. TATTGOC is not strictly a review site, though. We write about the whole experience of the night: the food, the people, the atmosphere ...

Whether it's a TATTGOC night or not, our favourite pubs include The Doublet, a wee place tucked away by the River Kelvin with a cosy lounge bar upstairs. We also absolutely love The Laurieston, a pub run by brothers James and John in the Southside. They've maintained it exactly as it was in the 1960s and it's one of the most relaxing places in the city. We're developing a taste for real ale as we get older, and The Three Judges in Partick has won countless awards for its range of beers and great service. Finally, if we're in need of a last pint in the city centre after a curry outing, we like The Old Hairdresser's on Renfield Lane. It doesn't open until 6pm but is a great wee hideaway near Central Station.

As well as curry, Chris loves vinyl and would recommend Mixed Up Records on Otago Lane which has an amazing selection of secondhand records. Monorail Music is great for new vinyl, a record shop housed within the Mono bar and vegan-friendly restaurant on King's Court. And we would both recommend a peek down Tontine Lane in the Merchant City. It's a tucked-away sidestreet that's essentially an outdoor gallery for neon signs and art installations."

See The Locals' Directory on page 136 for Graeme and Chris' top tips.

Follow Graeme and Chris' adventures on the TATTGOC blog here: www.trampyandthetramp.com

Chris: The Shish Mahal –
60-68 Park Road

Consistently excellent and traditional (old-fashioned) food. You should order:
• Hasina lamb chops (it is a TATTGOC mission to find any lamb chops in Glasgow that are better!)
• Vegetable pakora (impossibly light, made with cauliflower and potatoes).
• Lamb korma (manages to be both creamy and spicy) with plain naan and basmati rice.

Graeme: The Wee Curry Shop
7 Buccleuch Street

Very small restaurant with a handful of tables, but very special. You should order:
• Their unbeatable lunch deal: two courses for 5.49, with a rotating daily menu.
• South Indian Chilli Garlic Chicken (spicy enough to knock your socks off, though it might affect any romantic plans you have later!)

Shish Mahal

get away from it all

When the endless whirr of the city gets too much, step back into these secluded spots to gather you thoughts, rest your feet and take a deep breath, ready to start all over again...

Green Day

Just outside of the city there's an embarrassment of riches in Pollock Country Park (2060 Pollockshaws Rd, Southside, Map beyond D2) where miles of open parkland and forests open out in front of you with the frankly awe inspiring Burrell Collection in the park's centre, housing ancient relics and fine art from every era, including some astonishing items from the Ming Dynasty – just catch a train or bus headed to Pollockshaws from the city centre. To the west sits Mugdock Park with endless rambling walks and incredible views across the Clyde valley – a bus to Milngavie (this notoriously confusing name is in fact pronounced 'Mull-guy') will take you there. And of course the majestic Loch Lomond with its woodlands, islands and small hamlets dotted round the water's edge is just a stone's throw away via a short train ride from Central or Queen Street Station.

Walk the walk

For a walk to the city centre and some amazing views, stroll along the Forth & Clyde Canal starting from Lock 27 (1100 Crow Rd, Anniesland) all the way to its end at Port Dundas (near Cowcaddens underground). At a leisurely pace it should take around three hours. On arrival, rest your feet at the Chinese Garden in Garnethill (Hill Street between Dalhousie St and Rose St, City Centre, Map B3), a peaceful haven of zen shrubbery slap bang in the centre of the city.

It's all so quiet... shhh.

Alternatively, walk a little further to the gloriously restored Mitchell Library (201 North Street, City Centre, Map B2). With nothing to bother your thoughts but the soothing sound of hushed reverence and cautious footsteps across polished marble you can use the city archives to trace you ancestors, gawp at some medieval manuscripts or get lost in the vast Robert Burns Collection, the world's largest collection of Burns-related material.

The hot, verdant palm houses of Glasgow's **Botanic Gardens** are a steamy indoor-outdoor way to escape the elements. Dive into the Begonia entrance, past the arid cactus and into the moist warmth of the mini rainforest, where all manner of exotic plants dangle overhead, transporting you to foreign climes without the rain (unless the sprinklers are on). (730 Great Western Rd, West End, t: 0141 276 1614, Map A1)

For a cosy cinema experience, pay a little more for a comfy seat in the **Grosvenor Cinema** on Ashton Lane where extra leg room and full leather couches will give a whole new meaning to 'the back row'. To warm your bones, take in a cup of coffee from the bar outside or make it Irish with a wee dram. (Ashton Lane, West End, t: 0845 166 6002, Map A1)

At **Oran Mor**'s *A Play, a Pie and a Pint* you get all of the aforementioned for a more than reasonable price in the salubrious and warm surroundings of this beautifully converted church. Plays by famous and lesser known local writers are guaranteed to be at least as entertaining as the grub and the swally*. The programme runs over the spring and autumn months but even when the stage isn't set the ground floor bar is one of the West End's favourite watering holes. And before you leave... be sure to check out Alasdair Gray's stunning ceiling mural in the auditorium. Find out what's on at www.oran-mor.co.uk (top of Byres Rd, West End, t: 0141 357 6200, Map A2)

* swally - an alcoholic beverage of your choice.

While **Kelvingrove Museum** is one of the city's biggest tourist attractions its magical gothic spires are never more atmospheric than when there's dark clouds brooding in the sky above, rain clattering on the roof and whooping wind rattling the doors. Take shelter among its myriad of exhibits, grab a cup of tea in the café and at 1pm (3pm on Sundays) head to the centre hall where the daily organ recital fills the building with hair-raising volume, it is truly awesome. (Argyle St, West End, t: 0141 276 9599, Map B1)

The illustrious but welcoming walls of **The Glasgow Art Club** are the best kept secret on Bath Street. Here Glasgow's cultural aristocracy enjoy fine food in the inviting dining room and, in keeping with the inclusive club mentality, are encouraged to share tables with fellow diners. The original fireplaces and wood panelling in the upstairs gallery make it the perfect place to dry off, warm up and relax when the heavens open. As a members only escape, you can join the club with the password, "We're here to see the exhibition" - it's the only way for outsiders to get in. (185 Bath St, City Centre, t: 0141 248 5265, Map B3)

Warm your cockles with a hearty pint in **The Wee Pub at The Chip**, a tiny bar decked out with welcoming wooden beams, stained glass and barely enough standing space to swing a cat. The smallest cubbyhole of the long-serving and much-lauded Ubiquitous Chip, on a cold day The Wee Pub is full to bursting with entertaining chat and warming bodies. (12 Ashton Lane, West End, t: 0141 334 5007, Map A1)

ON THE BOX

The blackly comic adventures of **Rab C Nesbitt** have become ingrained indelibly into the Glaswegian conscience and following a host of television comedy awards, everyone else's too. As the city underwent massive regeneration in the late 80's and early 90's, TV's unemployed Rab and Mary were the voice of a Glasgow underclass city officials were keen to stifle. And *"I'll tell you this, boy, I will tell you this…"* much of Rab's pontificating still holds true today.

TV sitcom **Still Game** followed two male pensioners as they bundled through life, finding ways to entertain themselves in their dotage with a wry, bittersweet wit capturing both the brutal sharpness but deep down warmth of the Glaswegian sense of humour. Watching best pals Jack and Victor floating down the Kelvin in an inflatable dinghy as their old age drifts past you won't know whether to laugh or cry.

BY THE BOOK

The Dear Green Place by Archie Hind

Archie Hind tells the story of Mat Craig, a Southside working-class Glaswegian who struggles to reconcile his dream of becoming an author with the day-to-day realities of paying the bills. And it isn't just 1960s Glasgow that makes it a difficult place to justify a creative career – Craig's own family are embarrassed by his ambitions. This is one of the best Scottish books of all time, and all the more powerful for resonating strongly with Hind's own life.

Garnethill by Denise Mina

Glasgow is a great backdrop to crime fiction, and Mina's award-winning debut invokes some of the city's classic characters and landscapes. Maureen wakes up one morning with more than just a hangover; her boyfriend lies dead in the room next door, his throat cut. She knows someone is trying to frame her by playing on a recent mental breakdown. But she isn't sitting still and embarks on an investigation to unmask the murderer – before the murderer gets to her.

We can't sing the praises of the **Kelvingrove Gallery** or the **Riverside Museum** enough and once you've had your family fill, here's where we'd recommend next...

Glasgow Spy Trail

There's been a murder. Hidden throughout Glasgow's West End are clues to this walking whodunnit. Download the case, follow the trail and unleash your inner sleuth to find the killer of art dealer Archibald Anderton-Hope! Covering Hillhead, Byres Road and Kelvingrove Gallery it's more poppyseed bagel than seedy underbelly but this family friendly trail is a great way to immersive yourself in the hustle and bustle of Glasgow's West End. Taking around 2 hours and covering 2 miles it's dead good fun. (www.treasuretrails.co.uk)

Xscape Braehead

If there's an exact science to finding the right mix of activities to please every type of family member then surely Xscape Braehead are on to it. Indoor snowslopes, climbing walls, freefall drops, crazy golf, bowling, educational soft play and laser games are just the tip of this very cool iceberg. Four miles from the city centre X marks the spot for an xtra special family day out.
(Kings Inch Road Braehead Renfrew, PA4 8XQ www.xscape.co.uk/braehead)

Scottish Mask and Puppet Centre

There's something quite unique about the Scottish Mask and Puppet Centre. Developed as a centre of excellence hosting a theatre, workshop space and museum it's a reminder of the empowerment and freedom that comes from masks and puppets. With regular shows, workshops and parties the Centre's passionate team are an inspiration to younger visitors and champions of the imagination of everybody who passes through their doors. (8-10 Balcarres Avenue, Kelvindale, Glasgow, G12 0QF www.maskandpuppet.co.uk)

mily

MAKlab

Freeing your imagination in a very different way is MAKLab, Scotland's first open access digital fabrication studio. This fantastic space allows everybody to access that tools, learning and machinery to make pretty much anything. Keep an eye on their website for family friendly workshops run in a range of activities helping to fuel the inventors of the future. Always worth popping in whilst at The Lighthouse to add to your collection of 'Wow!'s. (The Lighthouse, 11 Mitchell Lane, G1 3NU www.maklab.co.uk)

Glasgow Science Centre

The appliance of science has never been so much fun. Three floors of magical models, interactive experiments and exploratory exhibitions are all enhanced by enthusiastic and friendly staff. Scotland's largest IMAX screen and the twinkling of 9000 stars in the Planetarium draw equal exclamations of wonder and awe, making a return visit a fact of nature. For those planning to visit more than once or twice the Science Passport is the way to go. (Glasgow Science Centre, 50 Pacific Quay, Glasgow, G51 1EA www.glasgowsciencecentre.org)

Popstars recording studio experience

The Jackson Five, The Osmonds, The Righteous Brothers, Sister Sledge and even The Kings of Leon found time at the recording studio on family days out and now you can too. Whether fame beckons or not, Popzone provide a recording studio experience in Glasgow's city centre with two hours of studio time for up to 12 people. Star treatment doesn't come cheap but surely you have to speculate to accumulate? (Central Sound Studio 61 Berkeley Street Glasgow G3 7DX www.popzone.co.uk/parties)

drink and

A drink. A swally. A pint. A jar. A tipple.
A wee hawf. Glaswegians have names for
alcohol like the Eskimos do snow, each subtly
different, each with its own story. And what
a story. Glasgow's pubs and boozers are at
the city's heart – a place for chat, for stories,
for catching up with old friends and for
meeting new ones, for learning new things
and forgetting how many drinks you've had.
Whether you're looking for a quiet drink in
front of a roaring fire or glamorous cocktails
made from exotic ingredients you'll find your
perfect pub here, waiting for you with a glass
in hand – take a drink.

Bar 91   The Halt Bar

When you want to step right into the middle of a jumping night out walk through these doors, with party shoes on...

A curious mix of withered old drinkers and trendy young folk cram into **Variety Bar** where on a Saturday night it's often hard to find a place to stand let alone sit. On the weekend electro music starts calmly but slowly builds to a banging crescendo, gearing up the throngs amid fish tanks, ornate ceiling plasterwork and ambient red lighting. (401 Sauchiehall St, City Centre, Map B3)

Speakeasy and loudly in **Black Sparrow** where high volume tunes complement high end 20's decor. Hang out with a crowd who are totally with it and have been for years. Folks in here are cool as ice, supping on one of the many liquors on offer, blending in perfectly with the illicit feel of the bar's décor. (241 North St, City Centre, Map B2)

Official pro club pub to the neighbouring Sub Club, **MacSorley's** comes alive on the weekend, filled to the gills with after work drinkers and clubbers meeting up and psyching up for a big night. Eclectic techno will soundtrack a nice meal of pub grub too. Their mac 'n' cheese is the stuff of legend. (42 Jamaica St, City Centre, Map C3)

A favourite with west end students, **The Halt Bar** is always jumping. It's standing room only at the traditional walk-around bar while the small venue space to one side hosts well-attended local band nights. Not sure where to go next? Check out the posters and flyers for club nights in the week ahead. (160 Woodlands Rd, West End, Map B2)

Ugly but beautiful? We've only seen the latter here. Hip young scenesters and well turned out couples flock to **Brutti Ma Buoni**, a trendy but welcoming cupboard of a bar with a wall to wall selection of wines and spirits. This tiny venue fills up quickly on most nights of the week while the seats outside are particularly nice on a sunny day. (106 Brunswick St, Merchant City, Map C3)

Cosy, casual and created for comfort, the following choices are the city's dress down drinking dens...

Despite feeling a little like you've walked into the Mad Hatter's Tea Party, with its mismatching furniture and eccentric china, **Butterfly & Pig** is a pleasingly quirky place to go for a quiet weekday drink and to nibble on their home-fried crisps. Sleepy doormouses would be well advised to avoid on the weekend when the tea party becomes louder and busier. (153 Bath St, City Centre, Map B3)

Fancy a bite to soak up all this alcohol? Get down to **Bar 91** where you can feast on some of the best (and biggest) burgers in town - the chilli burger is seriously amazing. When the weather heats up the front windows of the pub disappear, allowing punters (and some of their beer) to spill out onto the street. (91 Candleriggs, Merchant City, Map C4)

Is a great bar made of the sum of it's parts or does a great bar come first and the parts just fall into place? It feels like the latter in **The Belle** where you're instantly at ease and then more so with a roaring fire, Brooklyn Beer on tap, the watchful eyes of two stag heads and a row of porthole mirrors. As you settle into the retro seats you might just catch a glimpse of the Twenty's Plenty signs outside. It's going to be a long night... (617 Great Western Road, West End, Map A2)

Dotted with lecturers and ad hoc tutorial groups, **Stravaigin** is a firm favourite of the university crowd but you don't need a PHd to wander in. This warm drinking den is softened with twinkling lights and reclaimed curios adorning the walls. If you're drinking upstairs keep an eye out for the low ceiling beams although the beer and good food will soon dull the pain. (28 Gibson St, West End, Map A2).

From being a place for meat to becoming the place to meet, **Velvet Elvis** is a converted butchers that's now one of Glasgow's most laid back bars. Brilliant burgers and mighty "mince & tatties" makes sure the meat legacy lives on. (566 Dumbarton Road, West End, Map B1)

The Belle　🔲Butterfly & Pig　🔲Uisge Beatha

Get in lane! Taking in the bright lights on Cresswell Lane

■Brel ■The Laurieston ■Cottiers

Despite changeable weather conditions and freezing cold winters outdoor drinking is more popular than ever. Here are the beer gardens worth visiting...

Behind the bustle of Ashton Lane, **Brel** hosts the best beer garden on the street. An excellent selection of quality continental beers makes it near impossible to find a spare patch of grass let alone a picnic bench during summer but persevere and you'll enjoy envious glances from lecture-bound students at nearby Glasgow University. (Ashton Lane, West End, Map A1)

Maybe it's the mixed crowd – office workers, aspiring writers and the odd nineties pop star – that makes **McPhabbs** one of Glasgow's most appealing watering holes. Weekends see this converted townhouse in Park jump for joy as its well oiled clientele pack onto the makeshift sun terrace to talk politics. (23 Sandyford Place, West End, Map B2)

Ever been to Glasgow Green and thought 'Wouldn't this place make an amazing beer garden!?' Well it does. In the far corner at the end of the unmissable Templeton Building sits the **WEST Brewery**. Granted it's only a small patch of the green, but what a patch! Glasgow's very own German brewery boasts award winning bevvys like the luscious St Mungo's lager. (Templeton Building, Glasgow Green, East End, Map D4)

Everybody needs good neighbours. Where better to find them then down the local? We've picked a handful of pubs that have been recommended by those living nearby.

Lecturers, musicians, aspiring intellectuals and wags* direct from The Stand comedy club all gather in **The Doublet** where traditional pub atmosphere meets 21st century regulars with tremendous results. Upstairs drinkers take note of the fast clock behind the bar that will see closing time come 10 minutes earlier than the rest of Glasgow. (74 Park Rd, West End, Map B2)

* A humorous or droll person; a wit.

With an appealing glass frontage, warehouse sytle decor and and great music, **Stereo** attracts a cool young crowd making it a great place for a quiet drink next to Central Station. Housed in the ex-Daily Record newspaper building designed by Rennie Mackintosh you can tick it off in your spotters guide while downing a pint.
(20-28 Renfield Lane, City Centre, Map C3)

Like a welcoming outpost to the Southside, **The Laureiston** has everything that is great about Glasgow. Obituaries and pieces from Glasgow's past adorn the walls and the owners James and John make visitors feel as welcome as the pub's regulars. Hard on the outside and soft on the inside, the curious are rewarded with a real Glasgow gem. (58 Bridge Street, Southside, Map D3)

Sometimes the most enjoyable nights out are in the company of just one other person, so whether you're catching up or making out here's where to head...

Those wishing to impress won't go far wrong in **Chinaskis**, a low lit bar with an impressive range of liquor, good food and a romantically leafy beer garden. The super cool music policy and laid back crowd give the place a relaxed vibe that's as intoxicating as the bourbon. Still trying to impress? For poetry pretenders, Charles Bukowski quotes are dotted throughout the menu, just make sure you do all the ordering.
(239 North St, City Centre, Map B2)

Hidden from the busy West End thoroughfare of Byres Road, **Cottier's** is a converted church that's a favourite with locals for its roaring fires, secluded beer garden and heavenly atmosphere. Any drama here takes place in the neighbouring theatre.
(93-95, Hyndland St, West End, Map A1)

For something a bit more cultural, **CCA** (Centre for Contemporary Arts) will see you right. Upstairs the bar (entrance on Scott St) may at first seem unremarkable but holds all the qualities of a great bar, attracting a party crowd on the weekend. The café bar on the lower level of this multimedia art space is ideal for a hassle-free daytime drink under a glass roof that's made for blue sky thinking (or grey sky drinking). (350 Sauchiehall St, City Centre, Map B3)

 The Doublet   Stereo   WEST Brewery

INTERVIEW: Janice Duffy
(subway driver)

I've been working with Glasgow's Subway for more than twenty years now. My twin sisters were already part of the company when I applied so I guess there's a bit of family history in the place which is not unusual – for some reason lots of different families seem to end up driving the trains.

I'm a very talkative person and spending four hour shifts driving in a cubicle wasn't easy at first. Luckily there's a bit of a sense of community in this job that makes going around the circle a much better experience.

Regular riders often knock on my window to offer me packets of sweeties and biscuits – old ladies are particularly generous!

It only takes 24 minutes to go around the line. It's a small subway, the third oldest in the world* actually, but it takes you pretty much anywhere you want to go. And if you're a visitor to the city, you're guaranteed to get something interesting at each stop, either a big attraction like the Botanics or a shopping area such as Byres Road. My favourite station is Hillhead Street; the cosy mews bars of

Ashton Lane are right next to it. Sometimes there will be live gigs at Oran Mor, the converted church around the corner – it really adds to the buzz of that neighbourhood.

There are a few characters to look out for next time you take the Subway; my favourite lot are Jack and Victor, the two policemen on the beat. They're like a comedy act really, and the nicest people you could ever find; we named them after the Still Game TV characters. And if you're really lucky you might bump into the Grey Lady – every now and then a gust of wind will travel through the tunnels leaving a whiff of lavender behind. A few people will swear they have seen this ghost – she used to be a clippie**, apparently.

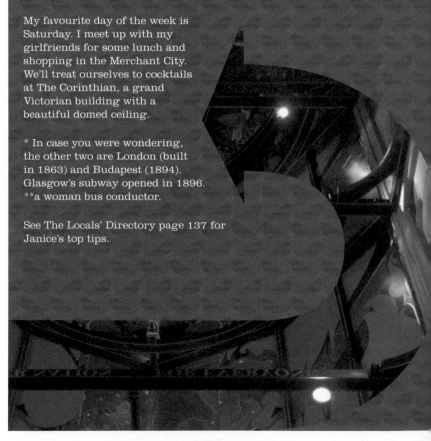

My favourite day of the week is Saturday. I meet up with my girlfriends for some lunch and shopping in the Merchant City. We'll treat ourselves to cocktails at The Corinthian, a grand Victorian building with a beautiful domed ceiling.

* In case you were wondering, the other two are London (built in 1863) and Budapest (1894). Glasgow's subway opened in 1896.
**a woman bus conductor.

See The Locals' Directory page 137 for Janice's top tips.

Choice destination of the more discerning Glaswegian, **Bar Gandolfi** is armed with all manner of classy concoctions to tempt the taste buds. Sitting atop sister restaurant Cafe Gandolfi, the building retains many of its original features reflecting its past life as a cheesemarket. Glasgow School of Art graduate Tim Stead's beautiful wooden furniture is best appreciated at night when illuminated by the stars under the glass roof. (64 Albion St, Merchant City, Map C4)

The unmissables

If you liked the movie Cocktail you'll love **Blue Dog**, where you'll find the best cocktails in the city. The crowd is more Bryan Brown than Tom Cruise with prices more Jamaica beach hut than downtown Manhattan. Combined with compulsory suave barmen and jazz pianists, the chances of you ploughing through extensive cocktail menu without falling over are slim. This place is a Glasgow cocktail experience all of its own. (151 West George St, City Centre, Map C3)

Reputedly the oldest bar in Glasgow, **Sloan's** must be doing something right. In fact they do lots of things right. From a fantastic collection of event nights to a tasty street food and sharing menus this alley cat has all the right moves. Don't forget to check out the ballroom on the second floor! (62 Argyll Arcade, 108 Argyle Street, Merchant City, Map C3)

Beside the Clyde you'll find two of the oldest pubs in the city. **The Clutha Vaults** (167-169 Stockwell St, City Centre, Map C3) and **The Scotia Bar** (112 Stockwell St, City Centre, Map C3) are jammed full of traditional character and Glasgow characters. Both pubs are renowned for their traditional live music which entertains lively crowds on the weekend though spontaneous singalongs around the piano aren't uncommon on any day of the week.

For a mini pub crawl head to **Ashton Lane**, a cobbled but bustling little thoroughfare behind Byres Road in the city's West End where pubs and restaurants line the street. As the warm days approach a holiday atmosphere develops and bodies pile onto the lane outside at the slightest hint of sunshine. Check out the pretty fairy lights in the evening too. (Ashton Lane, West End, Map A1)

Tall Ship, the Glen Lee admires its own reflection in the Riverside Museum of Transport and Travel

GET YOUR ROCKS OFF!

Whether you want to enjoy a bit of traditional fiddle music, check out the latest underground minimal techno DJ or catch big name bands playing in legendary venues, Glasgow is Scotland's one stop shop for live music. The city has a rich history of producing some of the biggest and best names in popular and alternative sounds, including Primal Scream, Franz Ferdinand, Orange Juice, Belle and Sebastian and The Vaselines (famously a big influence on Kurt Cobain). At grassroots level, the scene is in rude health – with over 20 venues and countless aspiring bands, you'll find at least two or three gigs on any night of the week. Here's a run down of the best venues and what you might expect to find there..

Too cool for school...

If you fancy hanging out with Glasgow's indie aristocracy, you'll find more than a few familiar faces and unfamiliar haircuts propping up the bar in **Nice 'N' Sleazy**, a long-standing epicentre of cool. Head downstairs for gigs and clubs in their tiny basement venue (421 Sauchiehall St, City Centre, Map B3). Similar crowds can be found behind the large warehouse windows of **Stereo** (20-28 Renfield Lane, City Centre, Map B3). For more intimate gigs from spoken word to performance art and everything in between, join the lines at **The Poetry Club**. Run by artist Jim Lambie, this former wing of SWG3 is a low-fi find. (100 Eastvale, West End, Map B1)

Lighting up the night and the night sky – the Barrowland Ballroom

A bit of history

Frequently name checked by bands here and abroad as the best venue in the world, going to a gig at the famous **Barrowland Ballroom** is an experience like no other. Due partly to its sprung floor and wide stage frontage (it's near impossible to have a bad view), this 2,000 capacity venue still retains all the nostalgic charm of times when waltzing couples would whirl under the glitter ball. The big, brash, flashing sign outside is a city landmark in itself. (244 Gallowgate, East End, Map C4)

Get spotted!

For aspiring bands climbing their way up the indie ladder, a gig at **King Tuts Wah Wah Hut** is a happy inevitability. Famously the spot (!) where Alan McGee spotted (!!) a young pair of Gallagher brothers in an early Oasis incarnation, King Tuts is a great place to spot (!!!) the stars of the future while rubbing shoulders with trendy locals. (272a St Vincent St, City Centre, Map C3)

The emperor's new clothes

A relative newcomer on the Glasgow gig scene, **ABC** is one of Glasgow's many converted cinemas resplendent on Sauchiehall Street and complete with the largest spinning mirrorball in the world. Inside two gig spaces play host to dazzling big name bands and shiny new artists as well as a roster of sparkly club nights popular with the burgeoning student population. (300 Sauchiehall St, City Centre, Map B3)

The weird and the wonderful

Looking for something a little different? When the night is right, the beautifully restored art deco **Classic Grand** is an almost incongruously classy place to catch some live music with exotic palms and mirrored bar surrounding the stage. (18 Jamaica St, City Centre, Map C3) A little further out of town, step into the country and western twilight world of the **Grand Ole Opry**. An average Saturday night will see cowboys of a certain age enjoying live country music mixed with line dancing, cowboy shoot outs and some surprisingly competitive bingo – in Govan real men wear Stetsons. (2-4 Govan Rd, Southside, Map D2)

YOU SHOULD BE DANCING, YEAH!

If a quick stroll down Sauchiehall Street on a Saturday night tells you anything it's that Glasgow likes to party. From glammed up girls tottering through Central Station atop towering stilettos to indie boys shuffling into King Tuts in dirty Converse, trendy fashionistas with asymmetrical haircuts hanging out in The Studio Warehouse to earnest students in The Art School, there's a place for everyone and everyone in their place. Here's a few choice cuts…

Dance, electro, house

Flying the flag for the Glasgow dance scene, **Sub Club** (22 Jamaica St, City Centre, t: 0141 221 1177, Map C3) is an integral part of the city's club culture. The tiny venue attracts big names to its regular weekly and monthly schedule while homegrown Sunday night club **Optimo** has achieved almost legendary status thanks to incendiary live sets and an eclectic playlist – forget about Monday morning, this is an absolute must. Located in the foundations of Central Station, **The Arches** (253 Argyle St, City Centre, t: 0141 565 1000, club entrance on Midland St, Map C3) hosts big monthly nights for techno/electro/house fanatics in atmospheric surroundings.

" I came here in 1990, just as Glasgow was celebrating its year as European City of Culture. I got British Rail to lend us an empty underground space in Central Station which had hosted a temporary exhibition. It was only meant to be for the three weeks of Mayfest but then I realised the council had mistakenly given us a 12 month licence. That's how we started The Arches.

I was unemployed with nothing to lose and saw the opportunity to produce theatre in small spaces, so I found a publican to run the bar and kept The Arches going for another year. It was a hand-to-mouth affair but those were really exciting times; we started club nights so we could fund our theatre operation and just like that Café Loco was born. It became a massive groundbreaking thing, a response to club culture. Except we did it differently. We had actors greeting people as they came in, large canvas on the walls for clubbers to paint, foreign films projected on the walls, some guys doing performance art in a corner. All this thrown in with a live band, some cabaret acts and a DJ. I didn't know it then, but we had created a new funding model for the arts, a club night that was paying for theatre! We got a lot of new audiences in and on the back of that the Scottish Arts Council gave us some money.

INTERVIEW: Andy Arnold

(Theatre Director)

After seventeen years at the Arches I moved to the Tron because I wouldn't want to do theatre anywhere else than in Glasgow - it has the best scene outside of London. Part of it I think is related to second-generation Irish immigrants

Andy at play not far from the Tron Theatre

who are so prominent over here; that knack
for storytelling which breeds good audiences,
people who admire the fact that you don't
use one word when you can use ten. Every
bit of humour is seized upon. And then there
was a great theatrical revival from the 1970s
onwards – unlike the rest of Britain, Glasgow
was picking up on experimental trends
popular in Europe, so the repertoire here was
very different.

The influence of this revival can be seen with
the emergence of a new breed of successful
Scottish playwrights. For cutting edge
performance head to The Arches, the place for
experimental productions. The Tron focuses
more on contemporary plays – new plays and
modern classics not seen in Scotland before.
The Tramway's programme emphasises
European performances and the place for new
visual arts is the CCA (Centre for Contemporary
Arts). Oran Mor has made its own mark with
their lunchtime theatre programme – head there
to catch a play, a pie and a pint.

See The Locals' Directory page 137 for Andy's
top tips.

See The Locals' Directory page 137 for Andy's
top tips.

Oran Mor; The Arches Theatre; The Tron Theatre; all
inside of this space do see The Tron's theatre programme
peek into Glasgow.

Indie and alternative

When is a club not a club? When it's **The Flying Duck**. You'll find all discerning indie clubbers here enjoying the laid back atmosphere and anti-club feel. (7 Renfrew Court, City Centre, Map B3)

When you should be dancing, yeah to even more live music, you should be dancing at **The Glad Cafe**. Another of Glasgow's great multi-arts venues, this cafe hosts everything from gigs, screenings, exhibitions and more. Whatever you're going for you'll be Glad you did. (1006 Pollockshaws Rd, Southside, Map beyond D2)

Cool and quirky venues

Home to Glasgow's fashion pack, **The Studio Warehouse** (also known as SWG3) (100 Eastvale Place, West End, Map B1) will take some finding but once you do the one off nights in this industrial warehouse club cum art gallery won't disappoint. In **The Art School** (168 Renfrew St, City Centre, B3), student union to the Glasgow School of Art, students of all disciplines and many more besides crowd onto the checkerboard dance floors, cutting shapes to Northern Soul, dirty electro and cheesy pop.

Find out what's on

Magazines **The List** (www.list.co.uk) or **The Skinny** (www.theskinny.co.uk) have all the latest club listings. Look out for flyers in pubs and shops too – you might find a couple of free or discount entry passes.

ROMANTIC GLASGOW

The Necropolis

Towering over the Glasgow skyline yet hidden away behind Glasgow Cathedral, The Necropolis is standing proof that in death as with life Glaswegians are image-conscious to the end (and beyond). Modest gravestones stand alongside outlandish merchant tombs and regal statues of city benefactors, designed by some of the city's greatest architects including Alexander 'Greek' Thomson and Charles Rennie Mackintosh. But you don't need to be a fan of the macabre to enjoy a romantic stroll past the resting places of the city's dead. Take a leisurely climb to its peak via winding paths past leering gargoyles and pious crosses and marvel with your loved one at the view from the top of the hill. There the city of Glasgow lays out before you nestled snugly in the cradle of the Clyde Valley. (Castle St, City Centre, Map C4)

Glasgow Film Theatre

Back in the 1930's there were more than 110 cinemas in Glasgow. The 1939 art deco Glasgow Film Theatre (known as GFT to the locals) was the first purpose-built 'art-house' cinema to open outside of London and is one of the few remaining picture houses still functioning as a cinema. Standing proudly behind the hustle and bustle of Sauchiehall Street this is the place to escape the crowds, settle down beside your loved one in front of a Sunday matinee and take in the old time glamour of 'Cinema City'. (12 Rose St, City Centre, t: 0141 332 6535, Map B3)

Loch Lomond Sea Planes

Really want to push the boat out? Sweep your loved one off their feet and into the skies for a flight with Loch Lomond Sea Planes. Anchored at Pacific Quay just next to the Glasgow Science Centre, this first class flying experience is the ideal way to take in the wonders of the West Coast of Scotland. 45 minute tours are around £140 but to make a real impression the special private charter is a must. For big spenders you can take a champagne flight for two to the banks of Loch Voil, dine at the award winning Monachyle Mor Hotel while your pilot awaits and return to Glasgow in style. The cost of lunch is not included, but with your head in clouds spending becomes so much easier! When money is no object romance is plane sailing. (www.lochlomondseaplanes.com, Map C1)

Botanic Gardens Riverside Walk

For a romantic stroll, look out for a small sign to the left of the toilet block in the Botanic Gardens pointing you towards a riverside walk. Follow the winding path down to the green banks of the Kelvin and the footbridge over the river, an ideal spot for Pooh sticks or amorous glances below the bustle of the street. (730 Great Western Rd, Map A1)

Glasgow University Cloisters

And if you can't get enough of that loving feeling... Wander through the gothic cloisters and quadrangles of Glasgow University's main building (University Avenue), enjoy the panoramic view over the Clyde from the steps at the bottom of Park Street South (West End), quaff oysters and champagne in the art deco **Rogano** (11 Exchange Place, City Centre, t: 0141 248 4055, Map C3) or wine and dine among resplendent mahogany in **Two Fat Ladies** at The Buttery. (652 Argyle St, West End, t: 0141 221 8188, Map C2)

A WORD IN YOUR EAR

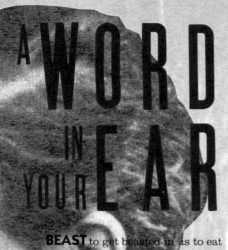

You don't need a phrasebook in Glasgow, just an attentive ear. To the careful listener the spoils of some of the greatest words and phrases in the English language. Selected from Michael Munro's fab book *The Complete Patter*, here are a few of our faves...

BEAST to get beasted in is to eat heartily and without standing on ceremony: 'There's yer tea oot boys – get beasted in.'

COORIE IN To cuddle or snuggle up to someone.

HEID-THE-BAW a nickname, sometimes affectionate, sometimes meaning an idiot: 'here he is, wee heid-the-baw himself!' 'this place is full a bloomin' heid-the-baws!'

MISS to miss yourself is to miss having a good time by not being present: 'Big Joe's party was rare, aye you missed yersel.'

PEELY-WALLY Pale, ill looking: 'Are ye awright? Ye're awfy peely-wally the day.'

HELL MEND YOU More or less equivalent to 'I wash my hands of you'. This is addressed to a person who despite all warnings continues in a course likely to bring trouble on his own head.

STOOSHIE a row, uproar, or brawl: 'There'll be a right stooshie when this gets oot.'

TORN-FACED Miserable-looking, wearing an aggrieved or hard done by expression: 'ach, ye kin dae nuthin right by that torn-faced aul crab.'

ANOTHER CLEAN SHIRT AN THAT'LL BE ME, you. him, etc. Used when someone is slightly ill (with a heavy cold for example); implies that the person is not long for this world; 'That's a terrible cough! 'Aye, another clean shirt and that'll be me.'

CAN'T SEE GREEN CHEESE Applied to a person showing envy or signs of wanting something just because someone else has it; 'naebody thought aboot a tracksuit till Ah got wan – yeez cannae see green cheese.'

RANDAN On the randan means a spree of debauchery, especially heavy drinking: No feelin sae good this morning/ on the randan last night, eh?

Pillars of learning...
the Cloisters of Glasgow University

Take a walk through the town on a Saturday afternoon, along Argyle Street and up Buchanan Street, past all the big name shops and a thousand Glaswegians getting a new outfit for the night ahead. Finding breathing space to browse can be tough but there are rails of calm out there if you know where to look. The city's quirkier, independent shops are often well kept secrets (you don't want to be seen wearing the same thing as someone else do you?) but, if you promise not to tell, here's where to go to stay one step ahead of the crowds. SSssshhhhhh…

■Cruise ▮Brazen ▯Princes Square

When it comes to stepping out in style, here are the lines, whichs and wardrobes we recommend getting lost in...

The price tags aren't for the faint-hearted but if you've got a hankering for high end and high fashion jewellery by top Scottish designers **Brazen** should be your first port of call. The beautifully designed shop shines on a less-salubrious corner of Merchant City like a diamond in the rough. (58 Albion St, Merchant City, Map C4)

A Grade A listed building and Scotland's first indoor shopping mall, the **Argyll Arcade** has been delighting shoppers since 1827. While big name brands have inevitably moved in, some of the smaller antique and specialist jewellers still retain that 19th Century charm as they cram their windows with precious stones and an overflow of diamonds. (Argyll Arcade, entrances at 30 Buchanan St and 102 Argyle St, City Centre, Map C3)

More a shopping destination than a shopping centre, **Princes Square** attracts top name brands and quality restaurants with its unique indoor-outdoor feel. Afternoon entertainment such as local choirs and piano recitals make it worth a visit even if you're skint, as does their always-impressive Christmas tree. (Buchanan St, City Centre, Map C3)

The eyes have it. At **Niche Optical Tailor** you won't come across any ordinary spectacle. Instead those peepers get the framing they deserve in this eyewear emporium that is the boutique experience your eyes have been waiting for. (119 Candleriggs, Merchant City, Map C4)

Fashionistas flock to **Cruise** for high end luxury fashion. Serving the city's style conscious since the 1980s this taste maker has always been on trend. Friendly in store stylists are the pleasant surprise for dapper debutantes unsure of where to start. (180 & 223 Ingram Street, Merchant City, Map C4)

Hats off to **William Chambers Millinery**. One of the stars of Glasgow's fashion scene William's award winning designs have been wowing the well dressed for years. Want to get a head? See you there later fascinator. (183A Bath St, City Centre Map B3 by appointment only: +44 (0)7815 096367)

A cut above the commoner casual options, these shopping spots combine funky flair with some elegant slumming...

In its wisdom **Fat Buddha** has filled a gap in the street culture market with everything from hard to find clothes labels, art & design books and a basement full of spray paints. The wall o' trainers is not bad either. (73 St. Vincent Street, City Centre, Map C3)

Whether you skate through the door on a customised deck or shuffle into the shop in well-worn Vans, street-savvy kids young and old will be welcomed into skater paradise at **Focus** which stocks exclusive brands like Nike SB, limited edition releases, rare imports and core skater favourites. (220 Argyle St, City Centre, Map C3)

Pick up a good deal at one of the city's many charity shops. To whet your appetite here are the must-see shops from our bargain hunting experts.

Within close proximity to Glasgow University, **Oxfam Bookshop** is the first stop for students eager to offload the previous year's set texts. As a result it can seem heavy on textbooks but a further look should uncover a few hidden gems and of course new students can find second hand course books on the cheap. (330 Byres Rd, West End, Map A1)

Vinyl hunters are lost for hours in the **Oxfam Music Shop**, both a charity shop and a terrific second hand music shop. Their range of 7" singles span from the 50's right up to the present day and there's even a few boxes of ancient 78s by the likes of Cole Porter and Fred Astaire. (171 Byres Rd, West End, Map A1)

The hardcore hunter makes **The Salvation Army** their first port of call. Reputedly the biggest Salvation Army store in Britain, there's tons to rummage through and bargains in furniture, antique items and clothes to be had. Early doors on Saturday is your best bet (91 Dumbarton Rd, West End, Map A1)

◨Niche Optical Tailor   ◨Fat Buddha

Rock down to... Electric Avenue. Royal Exchange Square at night

♩Oxfam Music Shop ♫Shop of Interest ♬Timorous Beasties

A parade of charity shops line the length of **Byres Road** and **Dumbarton Road** in the West End of the city. Proximity to Glasgow's wealthy inhabitants can result in some real finds at genuine bargain prices which continue to drop the further west you walk down Dumbarton Road towards Partick.

Come learn the art of shopping here

Located in the famous Rennie Mackintosh designed Glasgow School of Art, **The Glasgow School of Art Shop** houses goods by former art school students, including clothes, ceramics and jewellery. If you've got an eye for talent, you could nab yourself a future treasure.
(11 Dalhousie Street, City Centre, t: 0141 353 4526, Map B3)

Not quite a shop, **Glasgow Craft Mafia** are a collective of crafting designers and artists who make everything from edgy jewellery to trendy baby clothes. They host regular craft fairs often in tucked away venues in and around the city but they're always well worth seeking out. Details of upcoming events can be found on their website
(www.glasgowcraftmafia.com)

Spanning three floors of the Trongate 103 centre is the **Glasgow Print Studio**. Exhibitions, workshops and an excellent shop make this more than retail destination. Whether you are in the market to buy or to spy GPS will always point you in the right direction.
(103 Trongate, East End t: 0141 552 0704, Map C4)

Goodd shop showcasing the work of some of Glasgow's most exciting artists as well as being a haven for curious zine and niche publication collectors. As part of a perfect threesome, it's nestled next to Mono and Monorail music. (12 Kings Court, City Centre, t: 0141 552 6777, Map C4)

INTERVIEW:
KIRSTY WARK
(TV Presenter and Journalist)

Kirsty in the frame next to
FCB Cadell's *'Interior - The Orange Blind'*
at Kelvingrove Art Gallery and Museum

"My relationship with Glasgow begins through family roots. We lived in Kilmarnock but I used to come to Glasgow to see my grandmother. So many of my childhood memories are tied to this city – I remember it as a dark and sooty place with plenty of exciting things going on: hopping on and off the trams to watch the latest flick at the cartoons cinema, heading to Buchanan Street to look at Santa Claus and strolling around the parks. We would often take to Kelvingrove Museum on a rainy afternoon; as a child I was always terrified of Salvador Dali's painting, the Christ of St John of the Cross. My grandmother, in turn, absolutely loved it. For me the work of the Scottish colourists is the real highlight here. Particularly Cadell and JD Fergusson's paintings.

Glasgow is brash and loud and I quite like that side of it. I'm forever amazed with the building and landmarks of the city, there's a grandiosity that certainly inspired the model for other urban spaces – in the early 1880's architects came to Glasgow to see how its grid could be applied to the growing cities of America.

You can't truly know Glasgow without spending some time in the neighbourhoods talking to the community. I love meandering around Byres Road and Hyndland Road, where I do most of my shopping – Grassroots Organics is a wonderful supermarket and you can't get better meat than at James Allan. Delizique on Hyndland Street is one of my favourite delicatessens with beautiful home made food which you can try next door at Cafezique.

There are so many places that are close to my heart here and none more so than the Ubiquitous Chip, a restaurant my mother and father loved and where my husband and I got engaged. We still go there nowadays with our teenagers – the place is really connected to our sense of family."

See The Locals' Directory on page 137 for Kirsty's top tips.

A snapshot of Glasgow street style

Circavintage	Vintage Guru	Starry Starry Night	Mr Bens
A Ruthven Lane wonder with the 4 V's, vintage clothes, vintage jewllery, vintage accessories and even vintage textiles!	Affordable, open 7 days (and late on Fri and Sat) Jennifer and her gurus stock an ever evolving range of vintage wonders.	Even before you start browsing you know you've found something special on stepping inside this hidden gem.	There's not a decade left out in this emporium that's bursting at the seams with time-travelling treats.
Not Now Cato!	Isabella's Wardrobe	Barnardo's Vintage	The Glasgow Vintage Co.
With more vintage menswaear than most, Alan's labour of love showcases his stylespotting talent for guys and girls.	Not vintage but 'gently used luxury fashion'. Labels that have been loved and ready to love again!	Skimming the cream of second hand styles this charity shop swaps fusty for fashionable.	This classy store sidesteps clutter to give its clothes the space they deserve.
Saratoga Trunk	Miss Lottie Lou's	Retro	Glorious
Rails and rails of classic costumes and clothing to hire or buy. By appointment only.	Charlotte takes vintage fabric, vintage designs and crafts something new for you.	Student friendly shopping stop with an extensive range of 60s and 70s fashion.	A sprinkling of vintage treats amongst well loved high street repeats.

HILLHEAD BOOKCLUB

MISS LOTTIE LOU

RETRO

MARYHILL Rd

For Vintage treats and once loved wardrobe finds, Glasgow is a shopper's paradise. Here's a quick guide to you stepping in the right direction..

GLASGOW

THE GLASGOW VINTAGE Co

Still haven't found what you're looking for? Check out Granny Would Be Proud's Vintage and Craft Fair held three times a month at the Hillhead Bookclub. Get tae Facebook for the latest details.

SARATOGA TRUNK

BARNARDO'S SHOP

MR BEN RETRO CLOTHING

RIVER CLYDE

M8

■Caledonia Books   ■The Sentry Box

Banish inferior interiors and make your home beautiful from the inside out with a little help from these nest feathering friends

Iconic designers Alistair McAuley and Paul Simmons founded **Timorous Beasties** in Glasgow in 1990. The stylish window into their world in the West End gives you a taster of their work and if you're feeling particularly flush you can treat your home to some of their stunning wallpapers and fabrics. Big spenders come to talk about commissions while the budget conscious start with ceramics. (384 Great Western Road, West End Map A2)

Martin and May's beautiful shop in Finneston is a curated collection of local and international artistic and craft talent. Somewhere between a shop and a gallery **The Shop of Interest**… stocks homewares, jewellery fashion, prints and more. (1058 Argyle Street, West End, Map C2)

Shopping outside the box…

Staying alive, **Fopp's** spiritual home is on Byres Road. Long loved by locals this re-invented keeps it real with an excellent range of CD's, DVD's, books and all things music. Creaking floorboards are a happy reminder that this store has avoided most of the corporate upgrade underwent in other branches. (358 Byres Rd, West End, Map A1)

Fans of Black Books will rejoice on entering **Caledonia Books**, a second-hand book emporium with requisite dusty ambience and lop-sided charm. Explore through the back and upstairs to uncover a wealth of literary treasures on every topic but take note of the erratic opening hours. (483 Great Western Road, West End, Map A2)

Hidden just off the student thoroughfare of Byres Road, **The Sentry Box**, is a tiny toy shop to beat them all. A place of magical wonder for children and magical realism for adults, it's stuffed with bouncy balls, marbles, masks, crayons, glittery things, sparkly things and lots of wooden toys. A particular delight at Christmas. (175 Great George Street, West End, Map A1)

Mini chain **Love Music** is a poster covered indie record shop stocking dog-eared second hand vinyl, band merchandise and the newest releases most-wanted by the cool kids. It's also a good place to pick up flyers about upcoming gigs and club nights in the city. (34 Dundas St, City Centre, Map C3)

The Barras market is as renowned for its bargains as it is for some of its allegedly less than legal stock supply. Nonetheless a trip to Glasgow wouldn't be complete without a wander round its inimitable and incongruous maze of stalls and street vendors selling everything you've ever wanted and much more besides. (Gallowgate, East End, Map C4)

Suits you sir. Probably the most sought after tailor in Glasgow is the excellent **Steven Purvis**. In demand with Mods as well as the costume departments of Scottish Opera Steven's deft hands have made many a fine suit. Squeeze into his shop and treat yourself to an experience every man deserves. (8 Chancellor Street, West End, Map B1)

Keeping Glasgow laughing for over 100 years **Tam Shepherd's Trick Shop** is a treasure trove of treats from rubber chickens to exploding cigars. Small and perfectly formed this family run business always manages to see the funny side of things. (33 Queen Street, Merchant City, Map C3)

Stop, collaborate and listen. The patrons at **DeCourcy's Arcade** did just that and the result is a hub of great vintage and design stores with a funky teashop to boot. The curious shopper is rewarded with all sorts of treats as some of Glasgow's most interesting retailers set up shop just off Cresswell Lane. (Lower Floor, Unit 2, Cresswell Lane, West End, Map A1)

⚑The Barras ⚑Fopp ▣Tam Shepherd's Trick Shop

OFF THE BEATEN ATTRACTIONS

A trip to Glasgow isn't complete without a taste of some sweet treats from the fabled **Tunnock's Factory**. Better yet, visit Scotland's own Wonka Factory for yourself and see their infamous Caramel Wafers, Tea Cakes and Caramel Logs made in front of your eyes. No chance of getting the secret recipes though and visits are only available upon request – but be sure to book in advance, otherwise not even a golden ticket will help you here. (35 Old Mill Rd, Uddingston, t: 01698 813551)

Skip the queues and discover some of the lesser known treasures of Glasgow.

The **Hunterian Museum and Art Gallery** on campus at Glasgow University is home to much of the city's cultural and art heritage, including The Glasgow Boys collection, a multitude of works by the Scottish Colourists. And on Hillhead Street **The Mackintosh House** an entire replica of architect Rennie Mackintosh's home. The structural and interior design of the entire house has been replicated with the truly beautiful, all-white master bedroom a real standout. The house originally stood only 100 metres east on Southpark Avenue. On the exterior, keep an eye out for the house's curiously inaccessible front door, where at its original location the Mackintosh family could step onto the street but now a 7 foot drop awaits. (82 Hillhead St, West End, Map B2)

Step into the fifth dimension and experience the magic of the **Sharmanka Gallery**. Glasgow is now the adopted home of the sculptor-mechanic Eduard Bersudsky and the theatre director Tatyana Jakovskaya, founders of Sharmanka. Russian for Hurdy Gurdy, Sharmanka is a unique style of theatre, inanimate objects magically spring to life and the result is a performance that is captivating in detail. Sharmanka's magic is a gift to Glasgow. Go feel the kinetic energy. (103 Trongate, Merchant City, Map C4)

A trip to the **Britannia Panopticon Music Hall** is the closest thing to time-travel in Glasgow. The UK's oldest surviving music hall famously saw the stage debut of Stan Laurel in 1906 and has housed everything from wax works, freak shows and even a zoo. The ground floor is now an amusement arcade on Trongate but you can gain access to this piece of living history through a side door from Thurs – Sat noon to 4pm. You can also attend some of it's regular fundraising variety shows. Visit www.britanniapanopticon.org or call 0141 553 0840 for more details. (Above Mitchell's Amusement Arcade, entrance via New Wynd, 113-117 Trongate, Merchant City, Map C4)

The Elephant Under The Big Blue

In a city full of storytellers, it's a treat to get to hear so many urban myths. Illustrator and Glasgow School of Art graduate Eva Dolgyra created some stunning posters to tell these stories and this one in particular caught our attention. However, on further investigation, the legend of The Elephant Under The Big Blue became a mystery entwined with so many others that we found ourselves going around in circus circles in a search for the truth.

The story goes that under Kelvin Bridge next to the Underground lies an elephant carcass long buried. Its final resting place is just beneath a bar and restaurant formerly known as The Big Blue. And so the legend of the Elephant Under The Big Blue was born. Supposedly in the late 1920s or 30s the circus performing at Kelvin Hall would parade the animals through the West End on their way to the venue. On one occasion an elephant collapsed on the Kelvin Bridge and died. With no heavy lifting equipment to move the creature, a grave was dug below the bridge, one of the towers was dismantled and he was pushed into the river. There's apparently no record of this event and nothing to mark the grave. Subsequent swimmers and latterly Underground explorers have failed to turn up so much as a tusk.

This much we do know. There were elephants roaming the streets of Glasgow since the early 1900s. Processions of Chipperfields' and Billy Smart's circuses through the Gorbals became the stuff of legend with hundreds turning out to follow them through the city. Our elephant has also often been mistaken for another West End celebrity pachyderm called Sir Roger who was a Glasgow Zoo resident up to 1900. His remains were gifted to Kelvingrove where he has resided ever since. Even Loch Ness monster sightings have been explained away as travelling circus elephants taking a dip so the idea of the river Kelvin having it's own is perhaps not too far fetched.

Like the elephant, The Big Blue is sadly no longer with us and its new owners may know more than they let on having renamed the venue Inn Deep.

If you know anything about the Elephant Under The Big Blue please visit us at www.localsguidetoglasgow.com and tell us more. To see Eva's poster online and her other Urban legend posters please visit: www.evadolgyra.co.uk

THE BIG BLUE

The
CIRCUS
is in TOWN!

No Money

**Only got a few sweets and some fluff in those pockets?
Nae worries. Here's some cheap thrills in the land of the free...**

With 13 museums across the city, why not skip the queues and try something a little different? In the **St Mungo Museum of Religious Life and Art** (2 Castle St, City Centre, Map C4) you can relax in the zen garden or say hello to the Mexican Day of the Dead skeleton while Glasgow University's eerie **Anatomy Museum** (Thompson Building, University Ave, t: 0141 330 5871, Map B2, entry by appointment only), which features a collection of pathology specimens not for the faint-hearted. More fascinating than frightening, if you stumble into this working university library on a term day you'll find students revising their biology amidst jars of pickled hands and framed freeze-dried lungs. Ssshhh - no screams allowed.

Banish the Monday blues with **Glasgow's Blochestra**, an open orchestral gathering welcoming players of all ages and abilities to the Bloc Bar on Bath St. Founded by former Bloc barman Craig Carrick, this Monday night jam session has captured the imagination of drinkers and musicians alike with the orchestra now a fixture on the Scottish music festival circuit too. So dust down your trombone or just dander along to enjoy the Bloc rockin' beats. Visit their Facebook page for more details. (Bar Bloc, 117 Bath Street, Map B3)

Follow in the footsteps of Franz Ferdinand, Glasvegas and more as the excellent **Walking Heads Glasgow Music Tour** takes you backstage via the streets, bars and famous venues of the city. Guided by new music guru Jim Gellatly this downloadable audio app for iPhone and Android has a series of routes spanning the city giving an insight into why Glasgow became UNESCO's first City of Music. At around 50p a route it's going for a song! (www.walkingheads.net)

On a sunny day, get down to Kelvingrove Park where a range of sports facilities are offered gratis on a first come, first serve basis. Four synthetic **tennis** courts are up for grabs along with equipment (available to hire for a small fee) though it's best to book in advance during summer. Just over the fence, five **bowling** greens are available for keen lawn bowlers young and old while those with a more street edge will appreciate Kelvingrove's extensive **skate park**.
(West End, Map B2)

**Glasgow isn't branded 'Scotland with Style' fo[r]
Join aspiring socialites and the upwardly mobile
luxury destinations…**

High above the twinkling fairy light sky in Royal Exchan[ge] [a]re
you'll find **29**, one of Glasgow's finest private members club with
some of the plushest decor and most glamorous clientele in town.
Non members are allowed into some parts of the club, including the
much lauded restaurant but you'll need to sign up if you want to
enjoy the view from the super-exclusive, members only roof terrace.
(29 Royal Exchange Square, City Centre, t: 0141 225 5610, Map C3)

Chic West End gym bunnies go to **The Western Baths**, an ever
popular swimming destination since it opened in 1876. The
traditional pool remains, including swings and trapezes above the
pool, original high diving dale and restored viewing balconies above
for those unwilling to wet their ears although the plush sauna and
Turkish suite would be new to the Victorians. Non members can
also enjoy some of the venues facilities, including aerobics and yoga
classes. (12 Cranworth St, West End, 0141 576 0294, Map A2)

Hotel Du Vin's prestigious location at One Devonshire Gardens has
turned it into a byword for luxurious elegance in Glasgow. Its décor
really has to be seen to be believed while the in house restaurant is
one of the best in town. If you can afford to, stay here and follow in
the footsteps of A-listers that been before you. (1 Devonshire Gardens, West
End, t: 0141 339 2001, Map A1)

James Dun's House has quickly become *the* place to be pampered in
the city. After a long day shopping on Ingram Street, those in the
know take refuge in this Aveda Lifestyle Salon, where you can get
your hair done, relax with a massage, freshen up with a facial then
refuel in the cafe, all under one roof. (4 Hanover Street, City Centre,
t: 0141 248 5864, Map C3)

Poolhunter Robbie tests the waters at the Doulton Fountain in Glasgow Green

Scotland's rising swim star and 2010 Commonwealth Games Gold medallist Robbie Renwick feels totally at home in Glasgow.

"

I've moved to the city just after the Beijing Olympics to be close to the pool here at Tollcross and to study the University of Strathclyde. Knowing that the Commonwealth Games are here too makes it really exciting. It's nice to be part of it as you can feel the buzz in the city. With swimming it's a really early start in the morning and then we go back to the pool again for a few hours training in the afternoon. So how you rest and use your downtime is so important. I live on Glasgow Green which is a fantastic location for me. It's ten minutes to the pool and as quick to get to the Emirates Arena by car. I'm close enough to the Merchant City but also looking out on the park. I love the fact that despite being surrounded by a huge field it still feels like you are in the thick of everything. If I'm back from the pool I like to sit out on my balcony and watch people playing sports hanging out and enjoying the park. Being brought up on the suburbs of Aberdeen I've always loved being close to the countryside and being able to take my dog for walks along the river.

When I go for dinner with a group of friends we go to Pancho Villas, a Mexican restaurant in the Merchant City. The food's great, really nice. It's got a great atmosphere, really relaxed, really fun kind of restaurant. Doesn't take itself too seriously. It's where the squad usually goes for our Christmas dinner! For drinks my new favourite place to go with friends is a bar called Tingle which is down a side street near Buchanan St. The place is pretty small, usually has a great crowd, cheap drinks and a fun atmosphere.

Of all the things I recommend people seeing when I have visitors is Kelvingrove Art Gallery. I go there quite a lot in between training sessions and just wander around the paintings, historical exhibits, everything. You can get lost in there for hours. Afterwards there's loads of great cafes to grab a coffee in and then go for a stroll in Kelvingrove Park. If the weather's gorgeous and I've got a day off my favourite thing to do is to hop into the car and drive up to Loch Lomond. It's so close to the city and beautiful to swim in.

It's a brilliant city, there's always something going on in Glasgow, you're never bored. I love Glasgow more and more, the more I live here.

See The Locals' Directory page 137 for Robbie's top tips.

LOST LOCALS

Great people make a great city and you've got to meet some in the pages of this book. If we were time travellers here's a few of the lost legends we would love to have interviewed:

Oscar Marzaroli
Photographer
(1933 - 1988)

Oscar Marzaroli's evocative images of Glasgow spanning three decades from the 1950s are possibly one of the greatest records of city life anywhere in the world. Schooled in the city and having studied at Glasgow School of Art, Marzaroli worked as a photographer's assistant before travelling extensively in Europe and returning to Scotland in 1959. As a filmmaker he photographed extensively off set and on capturing everything from well known actors, writers and poets to everyday life in the city. It's impossible to sum up the visual impact of his images in words. All we can do is to recommend a visit to www. oscarmarzaroli.com, treat yourself to one of the many books featuring his work and see all sides of city captured by a man who loved it dearly.

Jimmy Reid
Activist, Politician, Journalist
(1932 - 2010)

The man and the mouthpiece behind one of the most famous moments in union history, Jimmy Reid (alongside Jimmy Airlie and others) co-ordinated the Upper Clyde Shipyard's work in of 1971 -1972. Faced with over 8000 job losses due to a withdrawal of government subsidy, Reid rallied the workers not to go on strike but to continue working to prove the viability of the shipyards. The subsequent climbdown from the Conservative government was an unprecedented victory for the workers and made Reid a household name. A natural orator he was one of the last great platform politicians having represented The Communist Party, Labour and finally SNP. Outspoken and passionate his talents and interests were wide and varied and the impact of his legacy continues to be felt in Glasgow and around the world.

Battling Betty
McAllister
Shopkeeper
and Campaigner
(1931 - 2009)

Betty McAllister was an true East End original. Her seafood shop on Bain St known as her 'office' became a HQ for community activism as Betty fought for people's rights in the Calton and her beloved

'Barras'. Not afraid to speak truth to power and with a keen eye for publicity stunts Betty fought numerous campaigns to improve the quality of life in the East End. Her direct approach included recreating road traffic accident scenes with children in bandages daubed with ketchup in protest at traffic rerouting proposals. These captured the imagination of the public, media and the ire of councillors and planning departments. Betty embodied the feisty spirit of straight talking Glaswegians and in 1988 on meeting Margaret Thatcher her immortal lines "Mrs Thatcher, you can stick the poll tax where the sun don't shine' summed up the mood of a nation.

Bud Neill, Cartoonist
(1911 - 1970)

Lover of westerns and the west coast vernacular, Bud Neil combined the two in series of cartoon strips that perfectly captured Glasgow's wry humor. His most popular character the Lobey Dosser was a Glaswegian sheriff in the Arizona town of Calton Creek populated entirely by Glaswegians. In the comic strip first printed in the Glasgow Evening Times in 1949, Lobey Dosser and his two legged horse Elfie duke it out with resident villain Rank Badjin. They're joined by a host of other characters including the G.I. Bride who with her baby Ned, is forever trying to hitch a ride out of Arizona back to Partick. With a love of the theatre, pantomime comedy and Glaswegian turns of phrase he created enduring characters who are still celebrated today. Lobey Dosser and the G.I. Bride are immortalised as statues in Glasgow's West End with the former being the only two legged equestrian statue in the world.

Mary Barbour Councillor, Campaigner
(1875 - 1958)

A woman who dedicated her life to improving the city of Glasgow, Mary Barbour was instrumental in organising the famous rent strikes of 1915. As many men left their homes to fight in WWI, unscrupulous landlords steeply increased rents in the city. In one of the largest protests the city had ever seen 'Mrs Barbour's Army' took to the streets and paved the way for the change in British law which restricted the power of private landlords. For Mary this was just the beginning and as Glasgow's first woman Labour councillor she campaigned successfully on a range of welfare issues, securing pensions for mothers, free school milk for children and she pioneered the city's first family planning clinic. Mary Barbour went on to be Glasgow's first woman magistrate where she continued to contribute to the well being of Glasgow's citizens.

Alan Pert

The People's Palace, Glasgow Green, Map D4

Rogano, 11 Exchange Pl, Merchant City 0141 248 4055, Map C3

The Steps Bar, 62 Glassford Street, Merchant City, Map C4

Public Toilets, 43 St Vincent Pl, City Centre, Map C3

Petra Wetzel

Glasgow Farmer's Market, moves between Queens Park and Mansfield Park, Map beyond D3 and B2

Mother India, 28 Westminster Terrace, 0141 221663, Map B2

Crabshakk, 1114 Argyle Street, 0141 334 6127, Map B2

The Left Bank, 33 Gibson Street, 0141 339 5969, Map A2

Cottiers, 93 – 95 Hyndland Street, 0141 357 5825, Map A1

Box of Delights, 127 Candleriggs, 0141 552 1875, Map C4

Glasgow Botanic Gardens, 730 Great Western Road, Map A1

Pollok Country Park, 2060 Pollokshaws Road, Map beyond D2

Mugdock Country Park, Mugdock, Milngavie Glasgow G62 8EL

Harry Creig

The Tenement House, 145 Buccleuch Street, 0844 493 2197, Map B3

The City Chambers, George Square, Map C3

Glasgow School of Art, 167 Renfrew Street, 0141 353 4500, Map B3

The Three Judges, 141 Dumbarton Road, Partick, Map B1

The Riverside Museum, 100 Pointhouse Rd, West End, Map beyond B1

Limmy

Cranberry's, 30 Wilson Street, Map C4

Firebird, 1321 Argyle Street, Map B2

Glasgow Botanic Gardens, 730 Great Western Road, Map A1

Trampy and the Tramp

Shish Mahal, 60 – 68 Park Road, 0141 334 7899, Map A2

The Laurieston, 58 Bridge Street, Map D3

The Old Hairdresser's, 20 – 28 Renfield Lane, Map C3

The Three Judges, 141 Dumbarton Road, Partick, Map B1

The Doublet, 74 Park Rd, West End, Map A2

The Wee Curry Shop, 29 Ashton Ln Glasgow 0141 357 5280, Map A1

Mixed Up Records, 18 Otago Lane, West End, Map A2

Tontine Lane, Merchant City, Map C3

Monorail Music, 12 Kings Court, City Centre, Map C3

Janice Duffy

The Corinthian, 191 Ingram Street, 0141 552 1101, Map C3
Ashton Lane, West End, Map A1
Oran Mor, Top of Byres Road, Map A2

Andy Arnold

The Arches/Cafe Loco, 253 Argyle Street, 0141 565 1000, Map C3
The Tron Theatre, 63 Trongate, 0141 552 4267, Map C3
The Tramway, 25 Albert Drive, 0141 276 0950, Map beyond D2
CCA, 350 Sauchiehall Street, 0141 352 4900, Map B3
Oran Mor, Top of Byres Road, Map A2

Kirsty Wark

Kelvingrove Art Gallery and Museum, Argyle Street, Map B1
Grassroots Organics, 20 Woodlands Road, 0141 353 3278, Map B2
James Allan Butchers, 85 Lauderdale Gardens, 0141 334 8973, Map beyond A1
Delizique (Cafe Zique), 70 – 72 Hyndland Street, 0141 339 7180, Map A1
Ubiquitous Chip, 12 Ashton Lane, 0141 334 5007, Map A1

Robbie Renwick

Pancho Villas, 26 Bell Street, 0141 552 7737, Map C4
Tingle, 33 Mitchell Street, Map C3
Kelvingrove Art Gallery and Museum, Argyle Street, Map B1
Loch Lomond is a 45 minute drive from Glasgow. Follow the A811 towards Stirling and ttake signs to the Loch Lomond and Trossachs National Park

VINTAGE TRAIL

Glorious, 41 Ruthven Lane, West End, t: 0141 357 5662, Map A1
Circavintage,37 Ruthven Lane, West End, t: 0141 334 6660, Map A1
Starry, starry night, 19 Dowanside Lane, West End, t: 0141 337 1837, Map A1
Glasgow Vintage Company, 453 Great Western Road, t: 0141 338 6633, Map B2
Saratoga Trunk, 10, 61 Hydepark Street, City Centre, t: 0141 221 4433, Map C2
Mr. Ben's, King's Court, 101 King Street, Merchant City, t: 0141 553 1936, Map C4
Not Now Cato!, Ruthven Lane Shops, West End, t: 0141 337 3877, Map A1
Granny would be proud: Vintage Fair, Hillhead Book Club, 17 Vinicombe Street, West End, t: 0141 576 1700, Map A2
Miss Lottie Lou, Upper Floor of DeCourcy's Arcade, Cresswell Lane, West End, t: 07583 633444, Map A1
Isabella's Wardrobe, 318 Crow Road, t: 0141 337 3877, Map A1

As well as the local legends featured in this guide we spoke to hundreds of people living in Glasgow to find out tips, secrets and recommendations to make the most of a trip here. Some of those tips have taken us online and as a result we totally recommend a visit to:

Hidden Glasgow

www.hiddenglasgow.com
From the unseen, yet to be seen and once seen this fantastic site is jam packed with stories and sights most might miss. The forums benefit from an active community of over 6000 contributors all keen to share their side of the city.

The Glasgow Story

www.theglasgowstory.com and
Our Glasgow Story

www.ourglasgowstory.com
These aren't the prettiest websites but they are a great example that a good story don't need dressing up. From a detailed background to the city to a rich selection of anecdotes and experiences on Our Glasgow Story, the curious come up trumps here.

This book has been many more years in the making than intended and hopefully is all the better for it. Thanks to our two designers; Claire Dowling who as a Glasgow resident set the tone and style, and Martin Elden who took the baton and ran with it by adding, enhancing and finding great ways to to tell Glasgow's story. Thanks to our first writer in residence Anne McMeekin proving that the Locals' Guide has legs by taking on the challenge and delivering a superb selection of the city's hotspots to get our teeth into. Thanks too to Julie McIntosh for her flavoursome recommendations. Massive thanks to our stellar photographers Matthew James Reid, Chris Gillies and Victoria Stewart whose images of the city and it's people have helped bring this guide to life.

We're incredibly grateful for the locals' who gave us their time, thoughts on the city and top tips. Alan Pert, AL Kennedy, Graeme Virtue and Chris Cameron, Brian Limond, Harry Creig, Janice Duffy, Andy Arnold, Petra Wetzel, Kirsty Wark and Robbie Renwick. Getting to know you and your Glasgow has been one of the most enjoyable parts of working on this guide.

Thanks to all of our contributors including illustrators;
Eva Dolgyra, Anna Kraay, Essi Kimpimäki, Nora Reid,
Mhari Baxter and Adrian McMurchie. The fab Flickr folk who gave
us permission to use their photos; Greg Neate, Graeme Bird, Andy
Cumming, Adrian Maldonado, Phil Dunsmore, James B Brown, Dale
Harvey, Gareth Morgan, Scott Ferguson, Laura Waddell, Helen M
Bush, Catherine Grant, Kirsty Orr and Stevie Spiers. Thanks also to
Michael Munro for permission to use words and phrases from his
book The Complete Patter.

An extra special thanks to Lesley Morton, Miranda Ralston and
Paul English whose passion for Glasgow helped re-ignite the
urgency needed to make this book a reality. To Lauren Cheape,
our intern, thanks for ideas, research and good publishing practice.
Thanks too to Iain Edwards, Jim Duffy and all at Entrepreneurial
Spark who helped maintain that momentum and provided support,
ideas and inspiration to take this adventure further. Cheers to
everybody for all the votes, donations and crowdfunding support.

Thanks to Vicky for proofing the Guide and doing it at such short
notice. Thanks to David Wishart and Craig Alexander at the Herald
for help putting faces to names, Lesley Booth for an insiders view of
GSA and to Alan at Not Now Cato! for the idea of a Vintage Trail. For
invaluable advice on map manipulation Bob Kerr at Openstreetmap.
Special thanks to Kim McGillivray for last minute illustration leads,
Kate George for the final final editing session and to Cathy Mclean
for giving me the free time to finish this book.

The Locals' Guide journey started in Edinburgh with Claudia
Monteiro and her passion for adventure and meeting new people has
been instrumental in laying the foundations for this guide. Thanks
Claudia for the kickstart that will guide many more adventures.

Finally thanks to my wonderful, ever patient and understanding
wife Vicky. Whether it's exploring Glasgow, getting lost in
San Francisco or just chilling at home every adventure is all the
better for sharing it with you and our beautiful daughter Delphine.

To good to leave out!

A-Ten-Shun!
For marks out of 10 you can't get any higher than this place. Small and perfectly formed Bar 10 is the perfect antidote to a day of city entre shopping. (10 Mitchell Lane, City Centre, Map C3)

That's life drawing Jim
...but not as we know it. In the relaxed setting of the Flying Duck Bar, All the Young Nudes is an informal sketching session taking place every Tuesday. Pencils at the ready! (142 Renfield St, City Centre Map B3 www.aytn.co.uk)

For the stein of your life
Beer and pizza is not just for nights in. Bier Halle's extensive 2for1 pizza menu goes best with friends and is one of our faves for city centre cheap eats! (7-9 Gordon St, City Centre, Map C3)

Tip of the Tongue
A place of pilgrimmage for music fans of the underground and avant garde Volcanic Tongue is a record shop with a difference. Sourced and curated by music journalist David Keenan, the hard to find will be found here. (The Hidden Lane, Unit 24A Argyle Court, 1103 Argyle Street, West End Map C2)

To good to Forget!

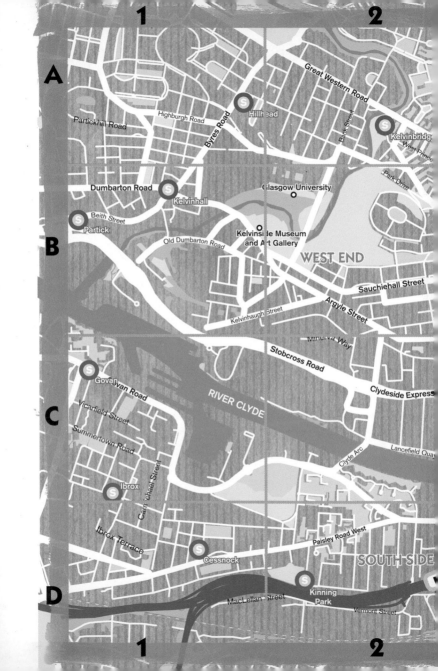